JESUS

IS THE GOOD
NEWS OF GREAT JOY
FOR ALL THE PEOPLE...

HIS LITTLE SHEPHERD
SINGS WITH JOYFUL LOVE,
HE HAS COME...
HE IS HERE...
JUST FOR YOU...
IN THE

HOLY EUCHARIST.

This Book
Jesus' Book

Is for every heart longing for Peace.
It was foretold thousands of years
Ago when a Lamb was sacrificed
And its blood was smeared on the
Doorposts and lintels to bring
Freedom and New Life for You.

The Second Pentecost is now
Descending on all humanity to
Transform and renew the face of
The Earth to become a New Paradise.
Where God will be loved and we...
Will love one another.

All because of a Humble and Beautiful
Virgin Mother who gave birth to the
Glorious Eucharistic Lamb of God.

MIRACLE OF ALL MIRACLES LOVE OF ALL LOVES

peter paul di cresce

Trafford
USA – Canada – UK – Ireland

The Scripture quotations are taken from the Holy Bible, Revised Standard Version, Second Catholic Edition 2002 Published by Thomas Nelson Publishing for Ignatius Press in 2006, and the New American Bible copyright 1976 by Thomas Nelson, Revised Standard Version, Catholic Edition, copyright 1987 Thomas Nelson Inc. ST. Jerome, New Catholic Study Bible. Thomas Nelson INC.

Order this book online at www.trafford.com
or email orders@trafford.com

Most Trafford titles are also available at major online book retailers.

Printed in Victoria, BC, Canada.

ISBN: 978-1-4251-6650-2 (soft)
ISBN: 978-1-4251-6651-9 (ebook)

Our mission is to efficiently provide the world's finest, most comprehensive book publishing service, enabling every author to experience success. To find out how to publish your book, your way, and have it available worldwide, visit us online at www.trafford.com

Trafford rev. 11/3/2009

www.trafford.com

North America & international
toll-free: 1 888 232 4444 (USA & Canada)
phone: 250 383 6864 • fax: 812 355 4082

DEDICATED TO

Jesus

WHO GIVES HIMSELF IN THE

HOLY EUCHARIST

PEACE TO YOU...
PEACE TO ALL...
IN JESUS WHO
IS RISEN, ALIVE
AND IS JOYFULLY
DWELLING...
AMONG YOU!

"The time is fulfilled, and the kingdom of God is at hand; repent, and believe in the gospel." Mark 1:15

PROLOGUE

It was my wise and saintly Spiritual Director, Fr. Venatuis Preske who suggested I write on the Holy Eucharist. In the 1940's I made a 30-day Ignatian retreat. The last meditation was on love. It was made in the chapel before Jesus in the Holy Eucharist. I was distracted the entire time and exclaimed, *"O Lord, what a lousy meditation."* Then, something happened. There was no need for faith.

I EXPERIENCED GOD'S PRESENCE IN THE HOLY EUCHARIST !

It was like being under Niagara Falls trying to pour all the water into a thimble. It was like thousands of volts of electricity going through me. It was awesome with great peace and joy. The Divine Presence was overwhelming.

No words could begin to describe it. It did not last long. All I could say was *"Wow!"* It never happened again. I live by faith. There is no desire for extraordinary experiences. The highest way to God is by faith. Living the Gospel, with a simple, humble and joyful heart; empty of self and trusting in God's infinite mercy and love and by loving and serving one's neighbor. This is the way to go.

It is in holiness, the cross and suffering that will accomplish it all. Holiness is being one with Jesus. All is grace. God has a unique plan for you and our world. If we follow Christ, there will always be the cross and suffering. But oh... what love, peace, and joy. Love overcomes everything. Love accomplishes the impossible. Jesus, the humble carpenter of Nazareth, who is Lord and Savior of the world, is the Way, the Truth, and the Life. He makes all things new. **To Live is Christ and Life is Love.**

Pope Benedict XVI has called for presenting ***"the truth and the Gospel of Christ in a fresh, creative and appealing manner."*** He loves beauty. God is beauty itself. Fedor Mikhailovich Dostoevsky said, *"The world will be saved by beauty."* If everyone would come to know, love and serve Jesus, our Savior Lord and God in the Holy Eucharist it would be a totally different world. The purpose of this book is to make it fresh, creative, appealing, different and stimulating, with a variety of poetry, art, photographs and prose for easy reading.

May Jesus assist You in listening quietly to the Holy Spirit speaking to your heart, so God can help set a new direction in your life. May Christ in the Holy Eucharist give you wisdom and deeper knowledge of yourself with faith, hope and love in Him who really loves you. Jesus will give you a profound peace and joy beyond anything you could have ever dreamed or hoped for. Let's face it; we are all weak. But with God... all things are possible. As Mother Angelica of EWTN Television would always say,

"IF WE DO THE RIDICULOUS, GOD WILL DO THE MIRACULOUS."

PROPHETS FROM THE OLD TESTAMENT

THE PROPHET HAGGAI

"Then Haggai gave the Lord's message to the people:
"I will be with you... that is my promise."

"But now don't be discouraged, any of you. Do the work, for I am with you. When you came out of Egypt, I promised that I would always be with you. I am still with you, so do not be afraid." Haggai 1:13; 2:4-5

Eucharist

"THE SOURCE AND SUMMIT OF THE CHRISTIAN LIFE"
Lumen Gentium (The Church No. 11)

THE PROPHET JOEL

"And it shall come to pass afterward, that I will pour out my spirit on all flesh; your sons and your daughters shall prophesy, your old men shall dream dreams, and your young men shall see visions. Even upon the menservants and maidservants in those days, I will pour out my spirit." Joel 2:28-29

THE PROPHET MALACHI

"For from the rising of the sun to its setting my name is great among the nations, and in every place incense is offered to my name, and a pure offering; for my name is great among the nations, says the Lord of hosts." Malachi 1:11

THE PROPHET DANIEL

"I saw in the night visions, and behold, with the clouds of heaven there came one like a son of man, and he came to the Ancient of Days and was presented before him. And to him was given dominion and glory and kingdom, that all peoples, nations and languages should serve him; his dominion is an everlasting dominion, which shall not pass away, and his kingdom one that shall not be destroyed." Daniel 7:13-14

THE PROPHET MICAH

"It shall come to pass in the latter days that the mountain of the house of the Lord shall be established as the highest of the mountains, and shall be raised up above the hills; and people shall flow to it, and many nations shall come, and say: "Come, let us go up to the mountain of the Lord, to the house of the God of Jacob; that he may teach us his ways and we may walk in his paths." Micah 4:1-2

THE PROPHET HOSEA

"Whoever is wise, let him understand these things; whoever is discerning, let him know them; for the ways of the Lord are right, and the upright walk in them, but transgressors stumble in them.

Hosea 14:9

THE PROPHET ZECHARIAH

"Rejoice greatly, O daughter of Zion! Shout aloud, O daughter of Jerusalem! Behold, your king comes to you; triumphant and victorious is he, humble and riding on a donkey, on a colt the foal of a donkey. I will cut off the chariot from E'phraim and the war horse from Jerusalem; and the battle bow shall be cut off, and he shall command peace to the nations; dominion shall be from sea to sea and from the River to the ends of the earth."

Zechariah 9:9-10

THE PROPHET JEREMIAH

"Hear and give ear; be not proud, for the Lord has spoken. Give glory to the Lord your God before he brings darkness, before your feet stumble on the twilight mountains, and while you look for light he turns it into gloom and makes it deep darkness. But if you will not listen, my soul will weep in secret for your pride; my eyes will weep bitterly and run down with tears, because the Lord's flock has been taken captive."

Jeremiah 13:15-17

THE PROPHET ZEPHANIAH

"Shout for joy, O daughter Zion! sing joyfully, O Israel! Be glad and exult with all your heart, O daughter Jerusalem! The Lord has removed the judgment against you, he has turned away your enemies; The King of Israel, the Lord, is in your midst, you have no further misfortune to fear. On that day, it shall be said to Jerusalem: Fear not, O Zion, be not discouraged! The Lord, your God, is in your midst, a mighty savior; He will rejoice over you with gladness, and renew you in his love, He will sing joyfully because of you, as one sings at festivals." Zephaniah 3:14-18

THE PROPHET EZEKIEL

"I will give them a new heart and put a new spirit within them; I will remove the stony heart from their bodies, and replace it with a natural heart, so that they will live according to my statutes, and observe and carry out my ordinances; thus they shall be my people and I will be their God." Ezekiel 11:19-20

THE SONG OF MOSES

"Give ear, O heavens, and I will speak;
and let the earth hear the words
of my mouth.

May my teaching drop as the rain,
my speech distil as the dew,
as the gentle rain upon the tender grass,
and as the showers upon the herb
For I will proclaim the name of the Lord,
Ascribe greatness to our God!...

with finest of the wheat... and of the blood
of the grape you drank wine."

Deuteronomy 32:1-14

"The Lord your God will raise up for you a prophet like me from among you, from your brethren... him shall you heed."

Moses, The Prophet / Deuteronomy 18:15

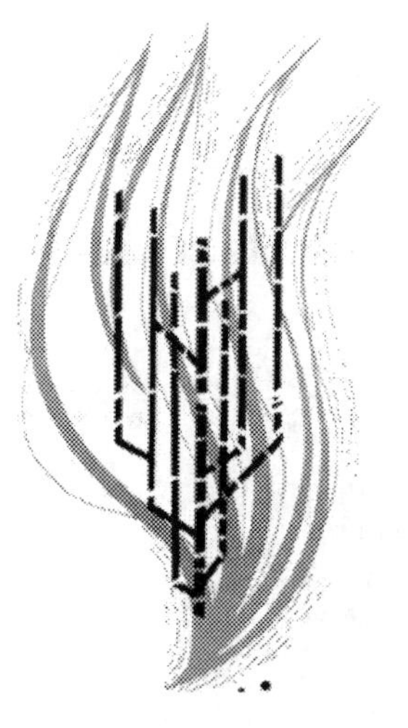

Why the
prophecies
of the
Twelve Prophets?
Because God speaks to us
Through the Scriptures.
The Old Testament is a
Preparation for the
Anointed One, the
Savior of the World.
Jesus came to fulfill
The law and the prophets.
On Mount Tabor, Jesus
Appeared with Moses
(The Law) and Elijah
(The Prophets). The
New Testament is
The revelation of God's
Immense love for all of us.
Jesus is Resurrected,
Living and alive.
He remains with us
Today in the
Holy Eucharist…

Speak Lord, your
Servant is listening.

THE PROPHET ISAIAH

"Lo, I am about to create new heavens, a new earth;
The things of the past shall not be remembered or come
to mind. Instead, there shall always be rejoicing and
happiness in what I create; for I create Jerusalem to be
a joy and its people a delight." Isaiah 65:17-18

CONTENTS

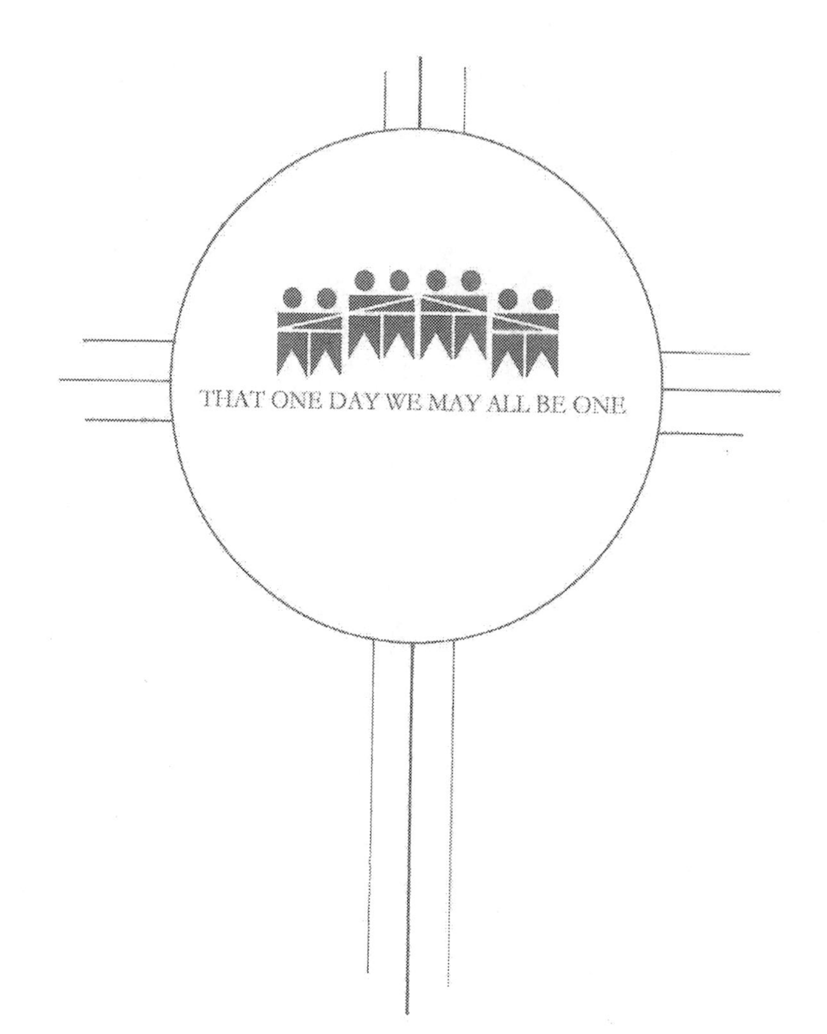

"...that they may all be one, even as you, Father, are in me, and I in you that they also may be in us, so that the world may believe that you have sent me."
John 17:21

"AND SUDDENLY THERE WAS WITH THE ANGEL A MULTITUDE OF THE HEAVENLY HOST PRAISING GOD AND SAYING GLORY TO GOD IN THE HIGHEST, AND ON EARTH PEACE AMONG MEN WITH WHOM HE IS PLEASED!" Luke 2:13-14

LEND YOUR EARS. LISTEN HUMBLY TO THE LORD'S INVITATION WHEN YOU VIEW THE SUN. ITS CREATION IS A VISIBLE REMINDER TO THE WORLD OF GOD'S GIFT OF HIMSELF

IN THE HOLY EUCHARIST

I CAME TO CAST FIRE UPON THE EARTH; AND WOULD THAT IT WERE ALREADY KINDLED!"

Luke 12:49

THE EUCHARIST

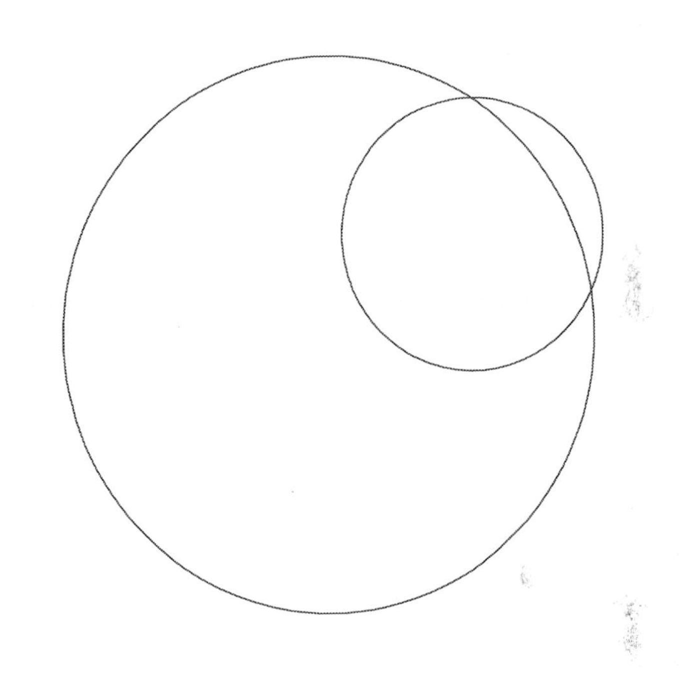

Is a call to conversion
Which is the means for
Transformation.

It is a call to restoring
The Unity among all
Christians.

The Sacred Heart of Jesus
In the Holy Sacrament of
Love is truly the Heart and
Center of the Universe.

The gift of Himself is His
Mercy which is God's
Greatest attribute.

It is a call to share and serve
The poor and all those in need...

IT IS A CALL TO LOVE

KISSING THE FACE OF GOD

In the poor, cold
Cave of Bethlehem
The House of Bread,
In the silence of the
Night, when the stars
Of heaven shone so
Bright as the Angelic
Choir sang their
Worshipping Gloria
In Excelsis Deo.

A beautiful young
Virgin Mother ever
So serene, wrapped
In a mantel of
Quiet, adoring love.

Her melting gaze of
Adoration on the
Precious newborn
Son of the Lord God
Most High, beginning
His reign over the
House of Jacob eternally.

Who will one day
Become her Eucharistic
Savior Lord, the tiny
Little Lamb of God
The humble, gentle
Savior of the world.

Nestled in the warm
Breast of the pounding
Heart of the Most Blessed
Among all women as she...

Kisses The Face Of God.

*"She gave birth to a son...
a boy destined to shepherd
all the nations with an iron
rod. Her child was caught
up to God and to His throne."*
Revelation 12:5

SONG OF THE SHEPHERD

How can it be what I see
Is He for real? What I see...
Is it a dream?
I am at a loss.

For lo and behold the most
Beautiful of all Mothers with
Her Radiant Infant of Light.

So Adorable...
So Holy...
So Lovely a delight.

I am only a poor shepherd
And have nothing to offer,
Yet I want to share everything
With You.

Having nothing to offer in
This world, Please...may
I give all my heart,
My life...
My self...
My humble love.

O Little Lamb
O Paschal Lamb
Of God...
The Holy One
The long awaited One
Manna foretold...

OUR LIVING BREAD FROM HEAVEN

"I have come in order that you might have life... life in all its fullness. I am the good shepherd, who is willing to die for the sheep." John 10:10-11

ONE AND ALL

The entire universe, the world
And all creation holds us spell bound.
Our wonder came into being from
Contemplating its singular source.

LOVE

How else to explain what makes
The world go round, or when a
Person falls in love it transforms
Every thing into love's joyful wonder.

As the heart rises up in song and in an
Ever ascending crescendo of deep gratitude
With praise for the gift of love that created
Us amazingly out of nothing.

The greatest Miracle of All Miracles, the Love
Of All Loves is an incredible act of supreme
Astonishment when love seeks total union
By becoming what looks like simple bread.

THE EUCHARIST

To graciously grace us each one and all
With Your eternal, burning, blazing fire as
We humbly melt, mesmerized in adoration,
Flowing into You, to become:

ONE AND ALL.

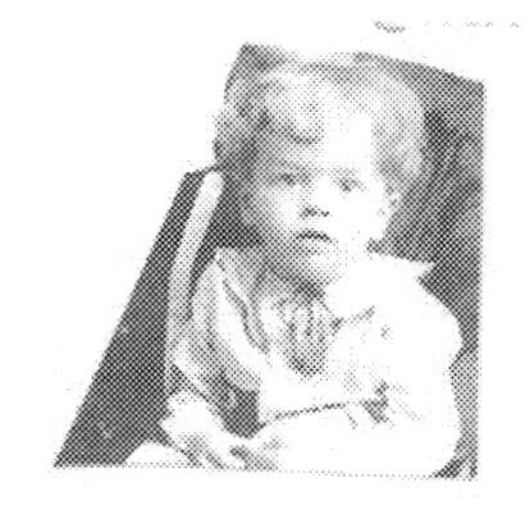

A LITTLE BABY BOY

A mother was holding her dear child,
A little baby boy with golden curly hair.
He reached out to me and his mother
Let me hold him.

Resting his face on mine, wrapping his
Arms around my neck, he just would not
Let me go. Every time his mother wanted
To take him back he declined.
She smiled and said,

"He has really taken to you."

*"Because I have just received Jesus,
and He is in me."*

It truly humbled me. Though I've held babies
Before, I never had an experience like this.
What a joy to hold holiness, purity and beauty,
Wrapped up in an adorable innocence.

I had been on my way to the Perpetual Adoration
Chapel after Mass when all this took place.

When adoring Jesus in the Monstrance, all I could
Do was to silently, humbly savor the overwhelming
Love that swept over me. Grace was bestowed
For it was indeed a gift from our Savior Lord,
For His love is overwhelming.

It has affected me deeply.

And now I have come to know why Jesus
Became a little Baby Boy...

To hold on to me and never... ever... let me go.

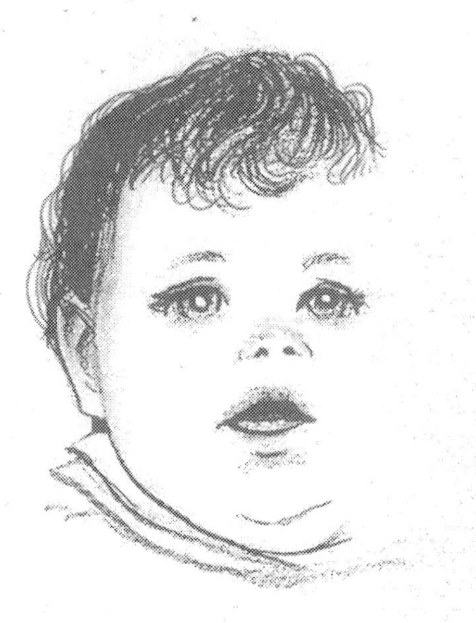

*"For a child is born to us, a son is given
Us, upon his shoulders dominion rests.
They name him Wonder Counselor, God
Hero, Father-Forever, Prince of Peace.
His dominion is vast and forever peaceful."*
Isaiah 9:5-6

When we were little kids we had heroes. Coming back from the movies we would play and pretend we were like the great heroes we saw. Well, the Apostles must have taken it to heart when Jesus told them they were to be like little children. And were they ever… those grown men arguing as to who was the greatest.

Haven't we done the same? How can we look down on them? So often we are concerned about ourselves. Are not the thoughts of the average person mostly about oneself. Most of us at some time or other have been centered in seeking to be noticed and or praised.

We admire heroes and great people. Those who are outstanding inspire us to be like them. Jesus, who knows all things, knows each one of us. Yet what is so amazing is that He wants each one of us to be the greatest.

Yes, you are indeed called to be great.

"Oh no… not me, that's impossible. You have to be kidding," is a typical answer.

"Unless you change and become like little children, you will not enter the kingdom of God. Whoever makes himself lowly, becoming like this child, is of the greatest importance in that heavenly reign. Matthew 18:3-4

"For man it is impossible but not for God. With God all things are possible." Mark 10:27

Anyone who loves the Lord Jesus seeks only to please Him, to do His holy will, and to develop a deep friendship with Him and live a Eucharistic life.

Spend time with Jesus in prayer and adoration and you will be like St. John the Apostle who was greatly loved by the Lord. You too will be called the beloved disciple whom Jesus loves.

"The greatest among you will be the one who serves the rest." Matthew 24:11

A LITTLE DANDELION

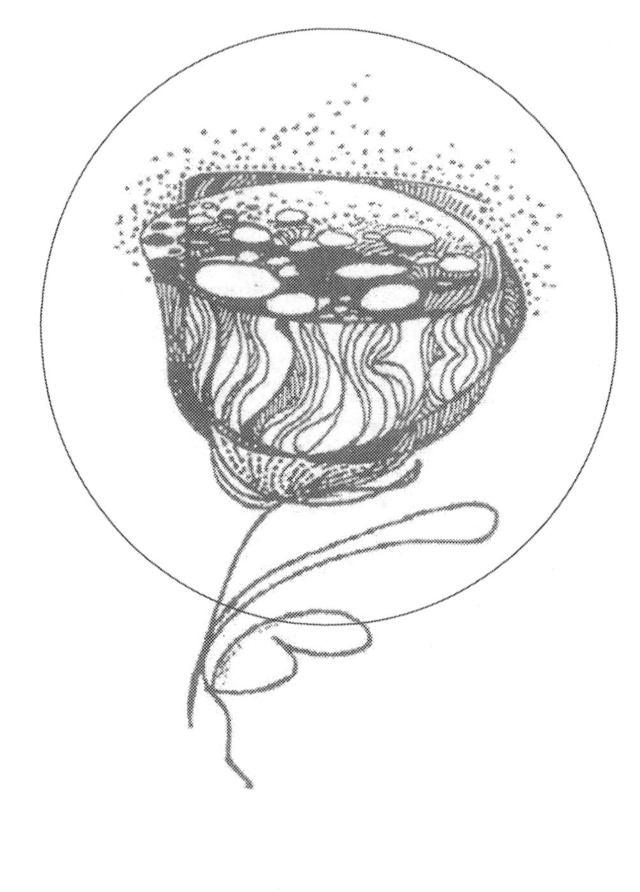

A little dandelion
Is so very special
Everywhere you go.
As far as you can see
There are myriads
Of these little golden
Flowers resembling
The radiating, golden
Sun in a quiet, common
And humble sort of way.
A joyful simplicity in a
Choir of golden faces,
Happy and joyful in a
Celebrating song of a
Sea of eternal springtime.
Singing their hearts out,
Praising their Creator.
Rejoicing in His beauty,
Basking in His gentle care.
In the air of Fatherly mercy,
Chorus of mirthful songs.
The mirrored image of
The mysterious, burning
Heart aflame, for us all.
Who leapt from the heavens
To humbly descend in the
Form of Eucharistic Bread.
Like countless little
Dandelions descending over
The earth as daily food of
Manna in awesome delight.
Now when gazing upon the
Beautiful smiling dandelions,
There is only praise and thanksgiving...

For I too am happy like a Little Dandelion
Transfigured into my Beautiful... Radiating Savior Lord.

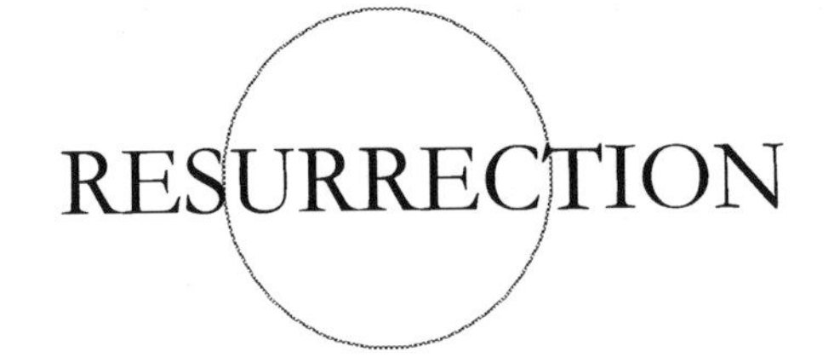

RESURRECTION

The shutters opened
Streaming brilliant light
In the radiance of the
Dawn's rising sun with
The effulgent rays
Dispelling the dark
As the Virgin's eyes
Well up with awe
Over the beautiful
And glorious sight
Of her Easter
Risen Son.

Basking in quiet peace
And gentle serenity
With arms wide open,
All wreathed in mutual
Tender looks of love

And melting in the
Fond and loving
Eucharistic embrace

Of a Resurrected Dawn
As all creation
Celebrates the Paschal
Joy in the beautiful words...

Behold I make all things new.

St. Augustine wrote that it is easy
to find Jesus in the Tabernacle and
He is there to comfort and listen to you.

TO DO SOMETHING BEAUTIFUL FOR GOD

Having experienced the pain, sorrow and agony
Of wandering nights and deserts, blinded in sight.
Always reaching out… forever grasping
For someone who cares, just a helping hand.

Mired in sands, hoping in vain,
Stumbling paths, blinding mists.
The raging storms in a cry of pain,
Of opportunities sorely missed.

Crying for help, pleading in tears
Burning within, struggling without,
Slamming of closed doors,
Doubting of what it's all about.

Storm clouds darken the mountains
Of woe, when all seems hopeless,
All fearfully lost, a living death to
Self… in darkness still.

Lo, the rising Sun radiating every
Thing new and bright. Song birds
Celebrating the Resurrection Dawn.

Reaching out to help the poor and needy.
Caring and seeking to give and serve others.
To each his own, at last… I have found true love.

Harmonizing music opening wide
The Door to do something Beautiful
For God, Our Eucharistic Savior Lord.

Oh My Beloved…
Your dreams….
And so much…
Much… more!

JACINTA

The first time I saw Jacinta, she was coming back from having Received Holy Communion, a beautiful soul carrying Jesus in the Holy Eucharist. Her natural beauty was transformed with a radiating, quiet and humble demeanor.

Beyond anything I could have dreamed or hoped for, God has given me precious gifts for my life... my beautiful Bride and our beloved Daughters, Joy Christie and Juanita. Jacinta is a beautiful person. Her great interest and joy is to give, share and serve. At Pot Luck suppers she brings more than just one dish. She is a real people person. Her life is centered on others and how she loves them.

I have never seen anyone so generous and giving. She is always thinking of others. She wears many hats, a pioneer woman of old. We have never fought or argued, but there were a few times, I am sure, she could have merited a martyr's crown for exasperation. To have a spouse who is so good, kind, loving and faithful is a great gift of God. She was consecrated to pray for all priests, and then lost her frontal vision. A great cross, she never talks about it. Few people know it because there is no self pity and she is so caring and joyful with a childlike spirit. God is so good. Jacinta and I have always centered our lives on Jesus, Mary and Joseph who want all of us to be members of their Holy Family. What more could I say?

Jacinta is all love, simple and wise. She is humble, joyful, faithful, funny and generous. Behind every great wife is an exasperated husband. She is my friend, companion, confidant, buddy and wife. One who is loved by everyone. When people come to know her... they fall in love with her. I have never been jealous because she is truly good and faithful. To know her is to love her. This is what heaven is all about. Living in God, we will be intimately united with everyone, surpassing the most perfect marriage on earth. We will all be one in and with Jesus. We will love everyone with the very love of God and be loved by everyone in like manner. This is what Heaven is all about. For those who have not experienced this (for all love emanates from God) you will in Heaven. You will be absolutely astounded as to what God has in store for you. It is far beyond all imagination, hopes or dreams.

Jacinta is a gift from God. Our Lord said, *"Every woman is a part of my Blessed Mother."* What I have shared with you began with Jesus in the Holy Eucharist. Life in the Holy Trinity is what it is all about. It is a life of love and intimate communion, for we all want to love and be loved. Only in Heaven will it be fully realized when we are finally in the mansions above, where the sun never sets and where there are no separations or goodbyes. We are all one... in the very love of the Heart of Jesus in the Holy Eucharist. It began there and will end there, in the Lamb of God who will be on Heaven's altar with everlasting Glory in Adoration and Love.

LAND OF THE SUN

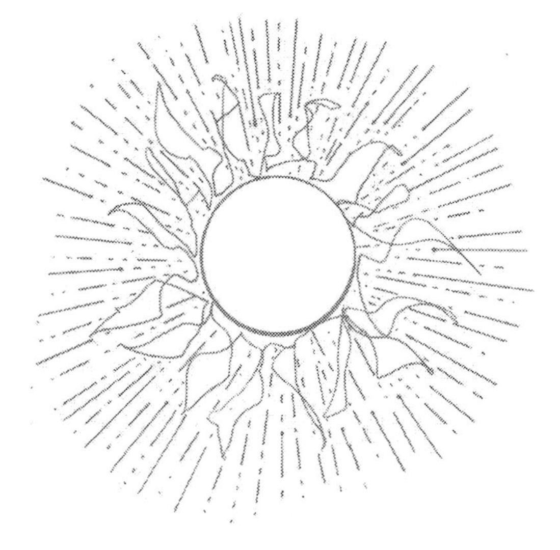

See the sun-kissed children of God, fruitful harvest of
The burning sands of Africa, land of the flaming sun.
Through ages of agony, suffering and tears, despite
Dignity and goodness, looking hopeless to everyone.

Beyond imagination and belief, Blacks suffered the
Ravaging slavery mingled with the blood of the
Lamb, the tears of the sacrificed Crucified One.

Out of hovels, out of slums, out of prejudiced
Hatred, poverty, and degradation… segregated and
Despised, the tears, fears and wailing sobbing cries.

Pleading for help, begging to be rescued from the
Jaws of inhumanity while clinging to straw in a
Drowning flood of utter abandonment… the dark
Night of sin and despair.

The people of the sun who walked in darkness have seen a great
Light. Those who dwelt in a land of deep darkness, a light does
Shine on the Land of the Sun. Our Savior Lord, God Almighty,
Has come to His beloved Black Children, resurrecting them,
Changing hearts, souls, and lives… freedom now won.

Hear the word of the Lord:

Children of the Land of the Sun will be radiating
Light to the world… becoming joyful children
Of the glorious and ever loving…
Jesus Eucharistic Son.

The world will one day glorify God Almighty who alone
Makes all His children beautiful in UNITY ONE.

"For a sun and a shield is the Lord God,
bestowing all grace and glory." Psalm 84:12

BEAUTY

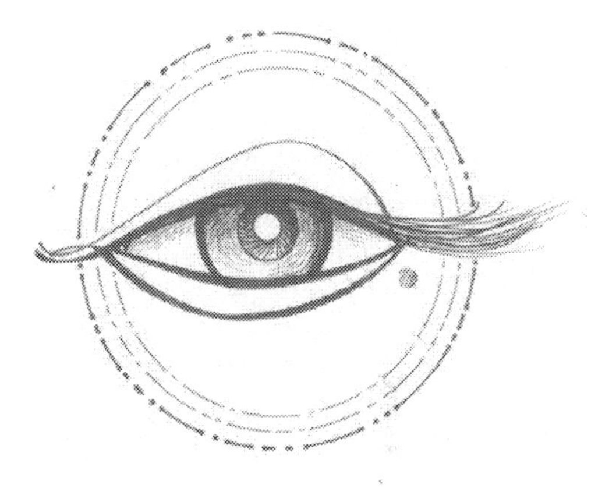

God has gifted me with the talent of being an artist. When
I was young I would think that if I were God I would have
Made every man handsome and every woman beautiful.

What happened? Looking at people, there are very few who
Are strikingly beautiful. I am always aware and attuned to
Beauty in persons, places and things. But the world, for the
Most part, is peopled like you and me.

Maybe sometimes we wish that God could have done a
Better job on us. When I was young I had a terrible case
Of acne. I cried and felt it was not fair.

When older and a little wiser, I realized how Good God is.
I know that if God had made me handsome, I would probably
Have ended up in hell.

Beauty is from within. Experience has proven that those
Who are ordinary, or were at the end of the line when
Looks were passed out, can have a beauty that radiates
From within. God's grace can do it.

You can be more beautiful than the movie stars if you
Let Jesus' light shine through you. In heaven everyone will
Be recognizable, but infinitely more beautiful.

So adore the beauty of Jesus in the Holy Eucharist
Who is Beauty itself.

**Imitate Jesus. Live the Ten Commandments and His Holy Gospel
Summarized in the Beatitudes and do His Holy Will in all things.
Then you will be one with Him to mirror His Beauty and His Love.**

WHERE OH WHEN?

Where, Oh When have I met You Lord?
Seen you, talked with you and listened in delight?
In all Your playful ways.
Concealing Your presence…
Unwrapping Your gifts,
One by one.
In the celebration of the altar
And by Your spoken Word,
In the color of the dawn
And candle lit nights,
Running through the flowered fields…
Listening to the roaring of the water falls.
In the strong clasp of
A friend's hand
Or a bobbing pony tail,
Always a smile wreathed in dirt.
Ohhh… the beauty of a face.
In the summit of the years,
The exchange of confidences
Deeply shared.
Mingled giggled laughs,
Sorrows, grief and pain untold.
The delicious aroma of bread
And burning leaves,
A flock of flittering sparrows,
The wag of a puppy dog's tail.
Ohhh Lord, My Lord.
Wonderful… wonderful…
You are hidden in
Uncounted ways.
And of all Your gifts
On life's Tree…
The Eucharist…
My heart leaps with
Joy…
Ohhh Lord
Your Image Fair.

THAT'S WHY

"Let's trade places."
"Oh Lord... You have got to be kidding."

"You have always said that you loved me."
"Yes, but you are God and I, I, I ..."

"Just trust me; it is only for a little while."
"But why?"

"Later on I will tell you why. Ok?"
"Ok Jesus, if that is the way you want it."

"Good, I knew you would."
"You mean, be in the tabernacle like you?"

"Yes, exactly"
"This can not be real. I must be dreaming."

"Father, I will it." (*The switch is made*)

"I can not believe this is happening.
It is so quiet... and Heh!... no one is even here.
I thought everyone would come.
Heh!... everyone... I am here!
Where are you? ... Where is everybody? ... not even one?"

"Lord... let's switch back. This is definitely not for me.
Jesus, you have been doing this for centuries... but why?"

"Because I love you beyond all measure and I want to be one with you...

THAT'S WHY!"

AFTER THE RAIN

Lo and behold, after a
Desert drought You
Opened the Heavens
With lavish outpouring
Rain. Now this morning
A paradise of bliss kissed
By the awakening sun.

In peace and tranquility
As birds merrily rejoicing
In a gentle cascading breeze,
Absorbing the re-birth of
Creation and arising anew.

Also within me… my Lord,
My Eucharistic God is my
Merciful Savior, the Living
Bread from Heaven who is
The Bread of Eternal Life.

Oh… my Beloved Creator
And awesome Artist God
With my Mother mine, the
Mystical Bride of my heart,
The Beautiful Blessed Virgin
Mary, with her Great St. Joseph
And all the Angels and Saints
We joyfully sing…

"My lover speaks; he says to me, 'Arise, my beloved, my beautiful one, and come! For see, the winter is passed, the rains are over and gone.

The flowers appear on the earth, the time of pruning the vines has come, and the song of the dove is heard in our land. The fig tree puts forth its figs, and the vines, in bloom, give forth fragrance. Arise, my beloved, my beautiful one…and come!"

Song of Songs, 1:10-13

St Francis and the Most Holy Body and Blood of Christ

"Kissing your feet with all the love I am capable of, I beg you to show the greatest possible reverence and honor for the most Holy Body and Blood of our Lord Jesus Christ through whom all things, whether on the earth or in the heavens, have been brought to peace and reconciled with Almighty God." St. Francis of Assisi

The Little Poverello, Your Beloved St. Francis, had a Tremendous love for You In the Holy Eucharist.

What a gift
What a treasure
How he loved You
Beyond all measure.
Truly meek and
Humble of heart
He lived for You
And became a
Living Gospel.
The Holy Spirit
Descended on him,
The power of truth.

Our Lady of the Angels gathered Him to her bosom In rebirth... Born again in The Lord... Another Christ.

PRAYER FOR PEACE

Lord, make me an instrument of your peace.
Where there is hatred let me sow love;
Where there is injury, pardon;
Where there is doubt, faith;
Where there is darkness, light;
Where there is sadness, joy.
O Divine Master,
Grant that I may not so much Seek to be consoled as to console;
To be understood as to understand;
To be loved as to love.
For it is in giving that we receive,
It is in pardoning that we are pardoned,
And in dying that we are born to eternal life.

St. Francis of Assisi

ARDENT DESIRE

In quiet, peaceful silence
Is Your majestic, glorious reign
Veiled in a lowly white Host.
Never a word, whisper or sigh
Not a sound, all in stillness be
As You speak in Holy Silence.

Jesus, in Your passion You remained
Ever quiet, despite the vehement
Accusations, mockery and contempt;
In silence You remained. But far greater
Were your ardent desires and love for us
And your enemies. Help us treasure silence.

As a gentle Peace permeates the air,
Drifting through the ages in joyful
Simplicity and lowly humility.

<u>You are Always There in the Eucharist</u>.

As One who always listens, serves,
Heals and grace bestows, radiating
A burning love beyond the human
Mind's ability to grasp or penetrate
The thoughts of Your ever loving
Sacred Heart.

Only to reveal the ocean's depth and
Mountain's height of Your yearning...
Burning to be with the children of
Your Creation... Redeemed and
Sanctified by our Savior Lord,
The Lamb of God who ardently
Longs for you and desires...

A Total Union of Love with You

The hardest thing in the world is for us
To realize that God's **ardent desire** is to
Work astounding wonders in and through
Us but, are we not blind and have yet to
Discover that we, not others, may be the
Main problem?

LOVE

Love is what makes the world go round.
It is the fire cast upon the earth.
Its source, the mystery of the heart.

The wonder of all wonders delighting
The eye, flooding the heart, birthing
Songs of love, radiating peace and
Transcending all that there is.

Who can penetrate its depths or ever
Ascend to the unending heights? For
Love's breath and purifying flames
Always harvests bounteous fruits.

Living life so true, fulfilling dreams
Beautiful, honorable, just and pure,
Lovely to behold…

For love is a person, His Sacred Heart
A fiery furnace, a flowing fountain
Of living waters, the effusion of the
Spirit transforming us by the
Living bread bestowing Divine Life.

EUCHARIST/LOVE…

IT IS ALL ONE

You say that you love God?
How much time do you spend
in prayer? Which is

Listening…

Talking…

Sharing…

So you say that you really love God?
Then how much time do you spend in
Adoring Him in the Blessed Sacrament?

**Jesus wants you to experience
the joy of loving.**

He waits and waits and will never stop
longing for you.

ST JOSEPH... THE GREAT ONE

There is a relationship between St. Joseph and the Eucharist. Joseph lived intimately with Jesus in His hidden life. He was not present when the miracle of the loaves and fishes took place. Nor was he at the Last Supper when Jesus changed bread and wine into His Body and Blood.

Ever selfless, he was the wise and prudent servant both faithful and honest. Joseph was a strong and silent man of prayer. Known for his simplicity and hard work, his deep faith inspired in him a humble and continuous adoration of Jesus, the Son of God.

Gratitude was a continuous refrain in the conversations of Mary and Joseph who lived a quiet and ordinary life with extraordinary love. Joseph is a model for all men. Ever faithful to duty he was a laborer with calloused hands who strove for excellence and did all things well.

Who can fathom the depth and intensity of Joseph's love for his Beautiful and Immaculate Virgin Wife, the Mother of God? His chaste love for her was exceedingly great. Its source was the love he had for Yahweh and His Divine Son. Joseph always sought to do God's will and to please Him in all things.

Like his namesake in Egypt, Joseph provided grain for God's people, but with the Living Bread from the Divine granaries for future ages to come. St. Joseph had a pure and joyful heart. The angelic husband of Mary was greatly loved and admired by Jesus and Mary.

Joseph lived totally for Jesus and Mary. The Gospels record not a word he said. A man of few words he had a simple and humble heart, and was a true gentleman. Ever kind, gentle and considerate he was solid as a rock. As Patron of the Catholic Church, know that he is yours too and also a faithful protector no matter who you are. Pray (talk) to him. He really listens. St. Teresa of Avila said, "I always receive whatever I ask of him." He is powerful.

Living a prayerful life of deeds, he had a profound love for the Sacred Scriptures. Acquainted with poverty, suffering and hardship, Joseph was refined like gold in a fire. Behind every great man is a great woman. It explains him well. Joseph and Mary were the first adorers of the Eternal Word of God, the Living Bread from Heaven. They lived a life of deep faith with beautiful simplicity and joyful love.

Pope Pius XII said, "If you want to be close to Jesus, go to Joseph."

ON FIRE

How many times have you read about fire in the Scriptures?

Fire is often used as a symbol of God. When Abraham, Moses, Solomon and Elijah offered animal sacrifices to God, fire fell from Heaven as a mark of His pleasure and acceptance.

How ironic that fire, which can be a symbol of God, is likewise the description of hell. Satan's aborted attempt to be like God ends in eternal fire.

The Apostles James and John wanted to call down fire from Heaven to consume the Samaritan village that refused Jesus.

He who is infinite mercy always responds with love, kindness and gentle forgiveness.

"I have come to light a fire on the earth. How I wish the blaze were ignited."
Luke 12:49

"He will provide relief to you who are sorely tried, as well as to us, when the Lord Jesus is revealed from heaven with his mighty angels; when "with flaming power He will inflict punishment on those who do not acknowledge God nor heed the good news of our Lord Jesus." *2 Thessalonians 1:7-8*

This speaks of the last day, His final coming. But, is not the Heart of Jesus a burning furnace of love? So immense is the love of our Savior that He gives you His very self in the Sacrament of the Holy Eucharist.

Jesus is calling us to help Him set the whole world on fire with His mercy and love.

Is there anything from preventing you from starting now?

THE ABIDING JESUS

At the Last Supper our Savior Lord offered Himself in His Eternal Sacrifice that is mystically present in every Holy Mass that has been offered daily for over two thousand years throughout the world, from the rising of the sun to the setting thereof, to take away the original sin… our sins, all sins, and to restore the Divine Life and grace lost by our first parents, Adam and Eve.

But He does far more. Under the appearance of bread and wine, the Living Bread from Heaven, the Holy Eucharist, Jesus gives us His very self to share His Divine Life in the Sacrament of Love.

Love seeks the beloved. Love yearns to be together with the beloved. Love never wants to be separated. Love shares. Love desires to be one with the object of ones' love. The Mass, the Divine Liturgy, is the re-presentation of the Eternal Sacrifice. In the Mass, you are actually in the presence of the Passion, Death and Resurrection of Jesus Christ, the Messiah, the Second Person of the Holy Trinity.

It is a mysterious and awesome miracle of God who makes you truly present on Calvary. Jesus who is truth tells us this very clearly.

God in His infinite love has made it possible throughout the ages till the end time for everyone to be actually present in His greatest gift to us all whenever we are present at a Mass.

"This is my body which is given for you. Do this in remembrance of me." Luke 22:19

What an incredible joy to have Jesus living in our very souls. How many times do we think about this? Is this what "pray without ceasing" and "always be thankful" is all about? Is not Heaven where God is? Oh how wonderful is this joyful and abiding presence of Jesus in our souls.

"If a man loves me, he will keep my word, and my Father will love him, and we will come to him and make our home with him." John 14:23

You who are the Way, the Truth and the Life… may we always be mindful of You in all our thoughts, words and deeds. May we joyfully abide in You. Jesus, we believe what You said in John chapter six of his gospel.

With Peter we also say,

"Lord, to whom shall we go?" You have the words of eternal life; and we have believed, and have come to know, that you are the Holy One of God." John 6:68-69

The abiding Jesus promises each one of us,

"And know that I am with you always, until the end of the world!" Matthew 28-20

MYSTERY OF MARRIAGES

A gift from God, our Father, the Sacrament of Marriage
Is an exalted mystery, like the Sacrament of the Holy
Eucharist wherein two become one and is the beautiful
Reflection of the life of the Holy Trinity. A Marriage
That truly lives a Eucharistic life is most fruitful.

Marriage is a participation in the Eternal Wedding Feast
Of the Lamb and it takes Three to have a Marriage
Pleasing to the Father: <u>The Two Spouses and Christ.</u>

THE FAMILY THAT PRAYS TOGETHER STAYS
TOGETHER was the recurring theme of the saintly
Father Patrick Peyton, the Rosary Apostle.

"And God blessed them, and God said to them, 'Be fruitful and multiply and fill the earth and subdue it..." Genesis 1:28

If a couple renounces themselves and lives for the
Other in following Christ by living the Gospel and
Carrying their Crosses, they will discover the fruit of
The Sacrament of Marriage is the Cross of Christ,
The source of all Christian life... the life of Holiness.

Marriage is the love and transformation of the souls
Into Christ. In Heaven, the love between everyone
Surpasses the most perfect Marriage on earth. Our
Lord said there would be no marriages in Heaven as
Everyone will be like the Angels with pure, seraphic
Love.

These marriage-like relationships emanate from the
Mystical Body and Bride of Christ, the One, True,
Holy Catholic Church to become All in All... one is
All in one in an everlasting Theophany of Love.

Because we will be in Christ and love everyone in the
Measure as the Eucharistic Heart of Jesus loves. He
Gathers us all into the very Heart and Life of the
Most Holy Trinity.

How beautiful a mystery is God's gift of marriage. Wherein Father, Mother and children. through The Sacrament of Marriage and the Holy Eucharist, truly become immersed in the very life Of the Holy Trinity.

THAT WE MAY BE ONE

I was in the Adoration Chapel when Jesus in the Blessed Sacrament was removed before Mass was being offered in the main Church. Everything was there but Jesus. It was empty and sad to see, even though it was only for a brief time.

It evoked a reflection on its symbolism. What would life be like without Jesus? It would be like the world without the sun, spring without flowers, life without a song, like an empty, dry and lonely desert.

It hurt to think of souls living in mortal sin without Jesus. What hurts even more is our beloved holy brethren who love Jesus and the Bible and have so much... but not Jesus in the Blessed Sacrament. Lord... help them to discover the truth in John's Gospel of chapter six.

Father, change our hearts and send the Holy Spirit to lead us all into the truth about the Holy Eucharist.

That there is only One God, One Lord, One Faith, One Baptism, and One Church... and He will remain with us like He said, until the end of time.

Listen, Jesus is saying to you now...

"GET HOLD OF YOURSELVES! IT IS I. DO NOT BE AFRAID!."

HOLY ROSARY

The battle of Lepanto was aided by the Church praying the Rosary, through the intercession of the Mother of God. We are gifted with the power of God in praying the mysteries of His life.

The prayer of the Rosary, in union with our beautiful Mother Mary, helps to contemplate the beauty of the face of God and to learn the depth of Christ's love for you.

In the humble recitation of the beads, we enter into the very mysteries of the Heart of Jesus. He helps us to be empty of self and with Him to live for others.

The Rosary was the favorite prayer of St. Louis De Montfort and Pope John Paul II the Great. They marveled at its simplicity and depth. They taught it had all the depth of the Word of God. It is praying the Gospel that contemplates the mysteries of Christ with Mary to foster a growth in holiness. Pope Pius XII called it a *"compendium of the entire Gospel."*

St. Louis De Montfort extolled the Rosary as *"the sanctification of the soul, the joy of the angels, the melody of the predestinate, the canticle of the New Testament, the pleasure of Mary and the glory of the Most Holy Trinity."*
"True Devotion To Mary," by St. Louis De Montfort, Ch. IV, No. 253

Pope Leo XIII, who wrote eleven encyclicals on the Rosary, said *"The rosary is an effective spiritual weapon against the evils afflicting society."*

Pope John Paul II closed his Encyclical on the Holy Rosary with, *"confidently take up the rosary once again. Rediscover the Rosary in the light of Scripture, in harmony with the Liturgy, and in the context of your daily lives."*

The Rosary is the prayer of the Word of God. It is meditating and immersing oneself in the mysteries of Christ, our Lady and the faith. Very powerful.

ON A SUNDAY MORNING

We were born again when you rose from the dead
On that glorious Easter Morn. You made all things
New with creation in a joyful song of ecstatic praise.
As we celebrate the Eucharist on Sunday, the Lord's
Day.

"Remember the Sabbath day, to keep it holy."
Exodus 20:8

Ah... the day of rest, remembrance of Your
Resurrection from the dead to free us and share in
The blissful life of God Most High.

Now each Sunday we set aside a day of rest to spend
With You and our Loved Ones in a celebration of
Thanksgiving and Praise for the Living Bread from
Heaven... Jesus in the Sacrament of Love.

With our Beautiful Mother Mary, her spouse,
The Great St. Joseph and all the celestial court
Of Angels and Saints. We... like little children
In simplicity of heart... sing, laugh and play by
Resting on the Holy Sabbath Day.

The rest of the story?

Just what part of the Sabbath Day is missing in
Your life and mine?

**If this is all about God's kindness in giving
Us a day of rest... what part does He play
In our observance of the Sabbath Day?**

ST. PADRE PIO OF PIETRELCINA

"Truly, truly I say to you, he who believes in me will also do the works that I do; and greater works than these will he do, because I go to the Father." John 14:12

Man of God
Humble priest
Friar who prays
Christ's confessor
Who forgave sins
Bearer of gifts
And signs of
Healing miracles
Ability to read hearts
Perfumed odor of Christ
Bilocation and prophecies
Gifted as his Father Francis
Of Assisi, he received the
Stigmata of Christ…
Jesus' five wounds
For over fifty years
Defying the laws of
Medical science and
Giving witness to
God's infinite holiness,
Love and mercy, who
Utterly lived for
Jesus in the Holy Eucharist.

"Truly Padre Pio is one of those extraordinary men whom God from time to time sends on earth to convert hearts."
Pope Benedict XVI

'May Jesus ever be the life of your heart, supporting it through every trial, transforming it into himself."
St. Padre Pio

FOR EVER MORE

In the quiet, peaceful stillness
Of the night, when all is in silent
Repose at 2:30 a.m., like Nicodemus
I come to You Lord.

It is really You Jesus. I adore You in
Wondrous awe. You are here. My
Faith tells me You are overjoyed and
Smiling with arms wide open.

I've come to be with You. How beautiful
You are. Those deep penetrating eyes of
The Word made Flesh, so luminous and
Beyond compare

A look of love, a melting glance
Overwhelms me with eager emotion.
You beckon me. My head is swirling,
My heart is pounding and no words
Come forth. They get in the way.

In Eucharistic adoration, I rest on Your
Loving Heart, so kind, humble, warm
And caring. Immersed in Your love.

Oh... if only I could bring everyone in the
Entire world here to rest on Your Sacred
Heart. This is living forever...

O PANIS ANGELICUS

Forever... forever... and FOR EVER MORE.

ON THE NIGHT HE WAS BETRAYED

In writing about the great miracle, the
Institution of the Holy Eucharist at the
Last Supper, St. Paul chose,

"...on the night when he was betrayed..."
1 Corinthians 11:23

Of all the words he could have used to
Describe the Miracle of All Miracles, the
Love of All Loves... Jesus giving us His
Very life, yet St. Paul starts out with...
Betrayal.

But why?

Maybe because night is a symbol of darkness;
Maybe because the greatest suffering of love
Is when it is betrayed.

Like when life turns to ashes, when beauty
Turns to ugliness, when fruit becomes rotten,
And when happiness is drowned in sorrow
Like a living death.

Who can ever fathom the Heart of Divine
Love?... Plunged into an ocean of infinite
Sorrow, suffering and pain... all from
The betrayal of One who is Love itself.

And I Lord...?

ST. JOHN THE BELOVED DISCIPLE

At the Last Supper... adoration's birth, John the Apostle
Reclined on the Heart of Christ, the ever burning furnace
Of love... the Lamb of God, the Son of God, Jesus the
Messiah, the Eternal Word of the Father who is love
Itself, the Source and Fountain of All Love.

Intimacy born of love. Faithfully standing beneath the
Cross. *"Woman there is your Son. In turn he said to the
Disciple, there is your Mother."*
John 19:26-27

*"Worthy is the Lamb who was slain, to receive power
and wealth and wisdom and might and honor and glory
and blessing!"* Revelation 5:12

Guardian of the Beautiful One, the Pure, Immaculate,
Holy One... Soaring Eagle, Mystic Saint, Evangelist of the
Word made Flesh and faithful Apostle to the very end.

Eucharistic disciple enflamed, revealing secrets of His
Pierced open Heart... through his spiritual gospel of
Life, Light, Truth, Love and the Bread of Life. When
Ancient of years, proclaiming the self-same message:

God is Love...Love one another.

Apostle John, you always say the same
Message over and over again!

**Little children love one another...
If you do this, it is enough, for it is
The Lord's commandment.**

*St. John appeared to St. Gertrude
in a vision and said, "Come Spouse
of my Master together let us lay our
heads on the most tender bosom of the
Lord, in which all the treasures of
Heaven and earth are enclosed...
Here is the saint of all saints;
All good things of earth and
Heaven are drawn hither as to
their centre."*

LOVE, PEACE AND JOY
Fr. Andre Prevot, SCJ
Third Edition Pg. 1
Tan Books and Publishers
Used with Permission

O BEAUTIFUL SAVIOR

Lord Jesus, how beautiful You are. O Beloved Savior, You are so gentle, kind and humble. O Lord, You Overwhelm us With Your love and mercy.

Like a little child I want to adore You because I love You. May I rest my head on You... to be caressed By You our Beloved God. You are our adoring, Wondrous Eucharistic Bread... our Peace, our Happiness, our Everything... and Our All.

With our Beautiful, Immaculate Mother Mary of All Nations. Mystical Bride of my Love... the Purest, holiest, ever Virgin Mother Mary.

And the Great St. Joseph, with myriads and myriads of angels who follow the Lamb where so Ever He goes... we worship and praise You, Eternal Word, Son of the One and Only God. With Seraphic angelic hosts and rejoicing saints we thank You, praise and bless You with simple, Humble, rapturous singing hearts. O most magnificent Living Bread from Heaven. We want to Be All in All in Your ever joyful, loving Eucharistic Heart.

You are the Savior of the World, the solution to every problem, the answer to every prayer Whether personal, family, community, national or international matters... simple or the most Complex, impossible geopolitical situations. Yes, including severe personal or world financial Problems that can lead to despair and utter abandonment of hope. Or even intractable cultural, Long existing conflicts and all the past horrors, brutalities and unjust historical evils that have Ever existed. You alone O Lord can give us the grace and power to forgive, respect, care and Help one another... both Individuals and Nations.

All power has been given to You in Heaven and on Earth. You still rule all nations and world Events. Help us to leave the interminable past and to help make it a New World because You Are the Father of us all. Truly You love every single man, woman and child on the earth.

You are the One and Only... Beautiful Savior of the World.

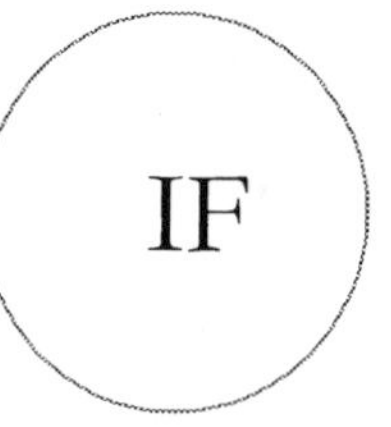

IF

If... you love Jesus in the Eucharist
If... you empty yourself and do penance
If... you practice virtue
If... you strive for a simple, humble heart
If... you confess your sins to have a pure heart
If... you always please God and do his holy will
If... when you fall down, you get up trusting in God
If... you are grateful for his mercy and grace
If... your life is centered on God who really loves you
If... your religion is in helping others
If... your piety is in giving, sharing and serving
If... you love Jesus in the poor, sick, lonely and elderly
If... you give of yourself in deeds, not words only
If... you always think of others
If... you live for the Church and not only for the world
If... you are a doer of the word and not a hearer only
If... you are truly humble like the least and the last
If... you are forgiving of enemies and those who hurt you
If... you are tough on self and easy on others
If... you praise, rejoice and live for God's glory
If... you are grateful, generous, giving and unselfish
If... you never gossip and everyone absent is safe
If... you are positive and have uplifting vocabulary
If... you can smile when it is hard to do so
If... you do not take yourself too seriously
If... you can keep a sense of humor when the going is tough
If... you never forget to say "thank you" and "please"
If... you know how to listen when others talk
If... you are a model of kindness and politeness and not a bore

Be Christ centered and not self-centered. If you fail with some of the above? Don't worry or look down on yourself. Simply go to Jesus and tell Him you are sorry. Ask Him for help. He will make up for your entire life, turning all your sins and failings into the gold of a New Child of God, a New Creature in Christ.

The Father loves you with the very same love as He has for His Son, Jesus!

SAINT JOSEPH

St. Joseph beloved of God and man. You had an incomparable goodness with a humility that radiated the aura of an angelic, childlike purity. How great you were in the eyes of the Lord God. Yet so simple and humble in a very ordinary way of life.

Like St. John the Baptist, you too were sanctified in the temple of your Mother's womb. You were the greatest soul that ever walked the face of the earth after the Son of God and His most Beautiful and Immaculate Mother Mary. You are the most Blessed of all men, chosen to be the chaste and faithful spouse of God's greatest creation, the ever Immaculate and Blessed Virgin Mary. A lowly and humble carpenter of Nazareth who lived totally for Jesus and Mary.

You were always filled with gratitude for your exalted grace and privilege, yet deeming yourself completely unworthy. St. Joseph, may all priests, men and boys come to know you and become stalwart pillars of virile manhood, virtue and holiness.

With strength of character and the sterling goodness of a simple, humble heart and a faithful honest life, may we become one with you, St. Joseph . You aspired to love and live for the Beautiful Blessed Virgin Mary and Jesus, our Savior Lord.

Our Lady, St. Joseph and the shepherds were the first adorers of the Infant Jesus laying in the manger in the town of Bethlehem, which means House of Bread. They adored Jesus, who would one day reveal Himself as the Living Bread from heaven... becoming the greatest gift and the most precious treasure on earth.

"If then you were raised with Christ, seek the things that are above, where Christ is seated at the right hand of God. Set your minds on things that are above, not on things that are on earth. For you have died, and your life is hidden with Christ in God. When Christ who is our life appears, then you also will appear with him in glory." Colossians 3:1-4

SINGING A BEAUTIFUL SONG OF LOVE

"O Beauty ever ancient,
O Beauty ever new."
St. Augustine

There is no one on earth
Or in heaven that can
Even begin to compare...
To the awesome Beauty
Grace and love in you.

In quiet humility and
Silence, we are at a
Loss and know not what
to do.

Yet as a little child we
fling our arms around you
and resting on your Loving
Heart...

Listening to the rhythmic
Beating of Your singing
Heart, the Beautiful Song of
"I love You."

Lita asked if I could do the entire book in my handwriting.
Though not possible, this page is complying with her request.
Lita is a beautiful soul who has a great love for the angels.

ROYAL PRIESTHOOD

Priests are chosen by God to the ministerial priesthood to preach the Word of God, offer sacrifice and sustain and nourish the faith of God's people. The Eucharist is the heart, center and life of our Holy Catholic Church. The priesthood of the faithful is little understood by the laity. Hopefully with more study, may there be a better understanding of this precious gift of God.

"...there is a diversity of service... the laity, too, share in the priestly, prophetic and royal office of Christ and therefore have their own role to play in the mission of the whole people of God in the Church and in the world..."
Vatican II Decree, Apostolate of the Laity, Ch. 1 No. 2

"You are a chosen race, a royal priesthood, a holy nation, God's own people, that you may declare the deeds of him who called you out of darkness into his marvelous light." Peter 1:9

God calls a great variety of men like the dignified, intellectually gifted John Paul II, Benedict XVI, Archbishop Fulton J. Sheen and many unknown Priests who are called to be other Christ's on earth. They are greatly loved by God and the Blessed Mother of Jesus. God wants all of us to be genuinely ourselves, but most importantly to be holy. Not only the ministerial Priests but also all the faithful are called to a life of holiness. The essence of priesthood is sacrifice. Sacrificial love is true love. The great vocation on earth is the Priesthood.

<u>The Eucharist brings unity, holiness and glory to God.</u>

Presently at this writing, Archbishop Sheen's life is being examined for possible canonization. He ranks as one of the great communicators of God's Word. Our Servant of God wrote 96 books by the time he went to his eternal reward in 1979. His last book was on the Priesthood. At the end of his life he wrote that the reason Priests fail is that they do not pray.

Anyone who does not pray will be in trouble. This applies to all of us because we are dealing with the spiritual warfare of the Principalities and Powers on high. St. Therese, the Little Flower, dedicated her life in praying for Priests. We too, no less, are also called to pray for Priests that they may be holy men of prayer and will faithfully read, study and live the Word of God, the Vatican II Documents and the Catholic Catechism. Hopefully all of us would do the same.

Though busy with their pastoral duties and obligations we pray that our Pastors and Priests, like John Paul II and Benedict XVI, Archbishop Sheen and St. John Vianney, will always be faithful to having daily Adoration of the Blessed Sacrament and when possible Perpetual Adoration, and support it by the example they give. We pray that they, like their Master, will be faithful and caring Good Shepherds of their flocks.

We will better understand the royal priesthood of God (ministerial and lay) when we have a deeper understanding and intimacy with our Blessed Lord.

O FATHER... OUR FATHER

Our Savior's life on earth was to love and glorify His Father. More and more, I am learning the secret depth of what Your name means to me, my Only and my All... my Abba Father God... my Messiah Lord the Eternal Word... Holy Spirit of Love... Holy Three in One God.

Be still... in quietness... and listen to Jesus and Our Father... within. Jesus, You are goodness itself. So gentle, kind, wise and caring. You overwhelm us with Your Forgiveness and Your Unbelievable Mercy...

O Lord, teach us how to pray.

For each one of us, with wonder and awe You made creation for us all. How You thrill us with wave after wave of fascinating and incredible beauty. Awesome is Your power, majesty and might. The panoramic clouds and myriad stars and the breathtaking sunsets and sunrises of the early morning light speak of Your never ending creativity and delight, for all is grace upon grace.

Lord, show us the Father. "...he who has seen me has seen the Father." John 14:8-9

The seasons reflect Your bounteous generosity in springtime, summer, winter and fall. The rapturous rose and the majestic Rockies enthrall us all. The golden grained wheat amidst the scented aromas of roses, lilacs and lilies after the springtime morning rain...how it reveals Your love beyond all measure.

Who can reflect the exuberant gifted goodness with no rhyme or reason? Wonderful, Your overwhelming love giving gifts upon gifts, wrapped up and ribboned with the beauty of Your incredible Creation.

The greatest of all prayers, the Our Father, asks for Supernatural Substantial Bread, the Holy Eucharist... as well as earthly bread for the body. Father, the fulfillment of all life and living is in Your will and Your love. Come one, come all, we are One Family in the One True God and Father of Us All. Let us sing, dance and be merry... praising our Father who is in heaven. O Gracious and Magnificent is Your Holy Name.

O beloved Father, You loved us into existence. You immerse us in a cascading waterfall beyond all imagination. Like the Divine Lover laying down his Life... Your Son's awesome sharing of His Eucharistic Love... to rest forever in Your arms.

The total transformation into Jesus is to make one's life a continuous act of love for the Father.

Ohhhhh Father... OUR FATHER

THE WAY, THE TRUTH AND THE LIFE

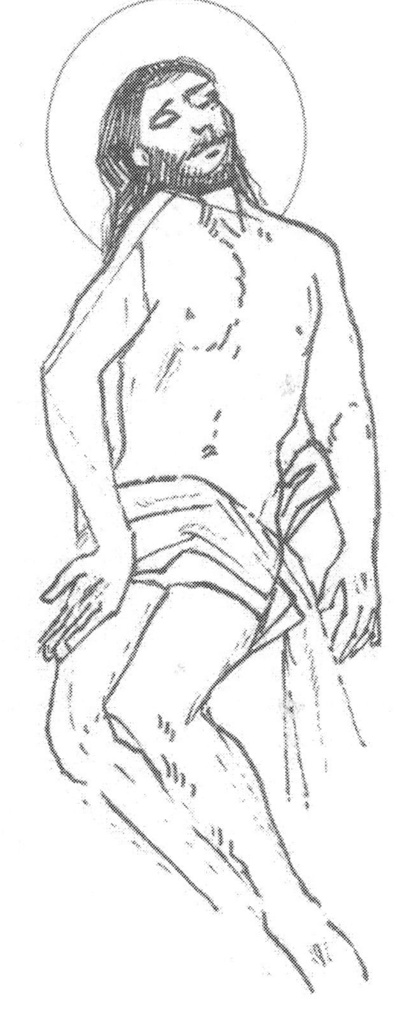

To reveal the treasures of His Sacred Heart, Jesus the Good Shepherd, told us He is the Way, the Truth and the Life. Our Crucified Savior Lord laid down His very life for you.

I AM THE WAY... the only Way that leads to the Father. I came forth from the Father to become man and make you one with Me. I Jesus, am the door you must enter to live a new life. I am in the Eucharist..

I AM THE TRUTH... The truth shall make you free. Truth is reality itself. Truth is humility. Seek the last place. Be simple, lowly and selfless and seek to be the servant of all.

I AM THE LIFE... The true life, the only life that lasts and never ends. Live a life of faith in Me. The invisible, unseen, interior life of Divine Grace that I give you by receiving My Sacraments from the Church I founded upon the Rock who is Peter. He is entrusted to preserve and keep the truth and the faith. You will live My life by living the Gospels, keeping the commandments and loving your neighbor. *"I am the bread of life."*
John 6:48

"I am the living bread which came down from Heaven; if any one eats of this bread, he will live forever; and the bread which I shall give for the life of the world is my flesh...truly, truly, I say to you, unless you eat the flesh of the Son of man and drink his blood, you have no life in you." John 6:51,53

"All this I tell you that my joy may be yours and your joy may be complete."
John 15:11

The Sacraments of Holy Eucharist and Reconciliation (confession) are linked together for a continuous ongoing conversion wherein we receive Jesus and the sacramental grace of forgiveness. Sacraments are the powerful gifts of God that come from the Body of Christ which is ever-living and life-giving.

FATHER TONY WILWERDING

He is like family to us. He is family to everyone...he belongs to the entire family of God. Father is tough, no nonsense, and his faith is solid like a rock. He was athletic and great with the young. Having a sharp mind he loved philosophy and studied it, but was bored and joined the Army as a Chaplain in two wars, Korea and Vietnam. At times, he served as many as 12 masses a day.

A man of the church, he is obedient to the Holy Father and the magisterium. **STYLE?** Father has the gift of bringing people together. His life is like a perpetual communion... just like his Master. **HIS GIFT?** He makes Church and religion appealing, like the real family it should be and is. He enjoys people, fostering community and friendship to better know one another. There are not many persons more generous, loved and respected than Father Tony who is a real people person.

Who said living a good Christian life was boring? Father remembers Jesus loved celebrations and wedding parties. He is a man of the Church, priestly and loyal to the Holy Father and his promises to the Lord.

His sermons are brief, starting out first with the reminder, "Pray the Rosary!" Almost 90, he has retired 6 times. Before his last **RETIREMENT...** he was helping at two parishes, visiting the sick, ministering to prisoners, visiting the sick in the hospitals, hearing confessions any time day or night and anointing and giving Holy Communion to the elderly in retirements homes. He is still having the Marian Movement of Priests Cenacles, and was Chaplain to the Legion of Mary, working with the St. Vincent de Paul Society and the Knights of Columbus.

Father Tony is close to his fellow priests and helps and supports them when he can. A Priest's Priest, he is still playing golf. **HIS SCORE?** He replies, "Lousy." A man of charity and kindness, he has a big heart and is always helping anyone in need. Tested by fire, he forgave those who ill-treated him, and forgave them with kindness. Never an ill word or unkind remark is ever on his lips.

He is always courteous with the good manners of a true gentleman. Practical and astute, he is gifted with wisdom, prudence and common sense. Father Tony is a man of few words. He is a listener and responds with brevity. For all his gifts and talents, he remains humble and treats everyone with respect.

HIS CHARACTERISTICS? He loves to tell jokes. People like to be around Father Tony who brings much joy and is gentle and caring with everyone. His generosity is legendary.

HIS SECRET? He spends a great deal of time with Jesus present in the Holy Eucharist and always prays his Divine Office in His presence. Father. Tony has a great love and devotion for the Beautiful Virgin Mother Mary, and like Pope John Paul II he loves to pray the Rosary.

THE ASCENT

Like St. John of the Cross, may
We strive to ascend the mountain
Of God.

Heart of my love, my very life
Why are You hidden?
The evening is shaded
Yet Your inner light
Gently leads me on
I know not where.

Hasten quickly, hasten
Together we shall run
Through the streams
Along the foaming
Waters seeking the heights
Of Carmel.

Up beyond the mountain air
High above the pinnacles
Scaling... climbing higher still
Sowing Your Word in
Its penetrating essence,
Overflowing the fountain
Of my rapturous heart.

As I languish in Your
Transfiguration more than
The brilliant glowing sun, blinding
My sight, darkly unseen
Yet burning with intense
Desires, piercing, wounding
The very depth of my soul.

Ah... when at last I'm
Gathered in the strength
Of Your unending embrace
As when I receive You in Holy
Communion, adoring Thy most
Holy... Radiating Face.

<u>The Sum of Perfection</u>

Forgetfulness of creation
Remembrance of the Creator,
Attention to what is within,
And to be loving the Beloved
St. John of the Cross

THE WEDDING

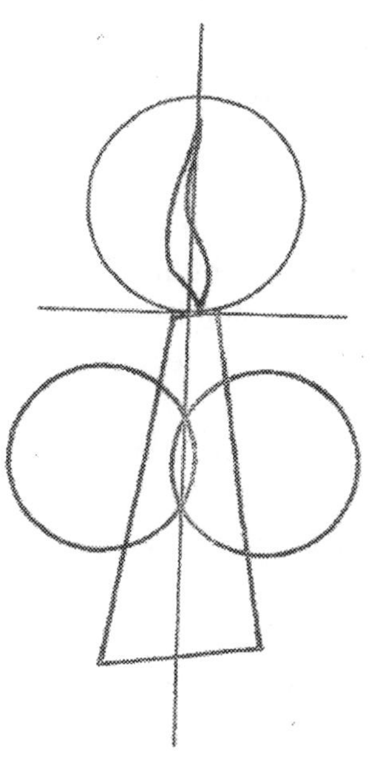

How many times Our Lord referred to the kingdom of God, that it is like unto a wedding. This is not a mere image but a Profound truth and reality. God has made marriage a Holy Sacrament. Our holy Eastern Rite Orthodox brethren call the Sacraments "mysteries."

Mysteries they are. For marriage is a reflection of an actual participation in the very life of the Holy Trinity. Jesus said,

"Is it not written in your law, I said you are gods?" John 10:34

You have existed from all eternity in the mind and heart of God who has loved you into existence. He longs to be so intimate with you that He is calling you to a total union with Him. It is incredible and unbelievable that the love and union He desires makes the life and joys of marriage a faint image of the happiness and glory awaiting you when you enter the heavenly mansion being prepared for you and your loved ones.

"Fear not, little flock, for it is your Father's good pleasure to give you the kingdom... be like men awaiting their master's return from the wedding." Luke 12:32

The Sacraments of Matrimony and the Holy Eucharist are reflections of Christ the Divine Bridegroom espoused to His Bride the Church. Living a sacramental and Eucharistic life will result in a fruitful, faithful and joyful married life.

All the members of a family participate in the priesthood of the baptized through prayer, receiving the Sacraments and living a holy life of thanksgiving, self-denial and genuine charity.

In imitation of the Holy Family of Jesus, Mary and Joseph, one learns the joys of mutual love, perseverance, generosity and the worship of God in prayer and living the life of the Gospel.

AHHH…O HOW BEAUTIFUL!

Ahhh, the beauty of a star stellar evening
Or the early awakening dawn of the
Glorious morning sunrise…gilding
Forever the traces left behind of the
Creator's soft touching footsteps.

In the wake of His exhilarating path
Leaving the mark of His signature
Everywhere; beyond what the eye
Can behold, ravishing the senses
In the overwhelming, melting joy
That intoxicates the heart.

Relishing the beauty of all creation
Mesmerizing the soul to its
Profound depths, yet it is only a slight
Intimation of the ecstatic beholder's
Discovery of delightful surprises.

For how could such beauty be so pervasive?
Everywhere…and ever increasing
To the fascination of the soul's
Vision…feasting, savoring, tasting,
As it contemplates the artistic creativity
That utterly enraptures the heart with
Emotions of supreme happiness.

Like the geyser of a sparkling fountain of
Musical waters in a symphonic splashing
Melody of…

A divine orchestration in unending
Discoveries, eternally reaching out
To the never ending source of the

Infinite Beauty of Holy Eucharistic Love itself.

I WANT TO LIVE

I want to live
I want to be free
I want it all...
It's all in Thee

I can't believe it and just
Laugh and sing. I've
Discovered the secret of
The life You bring.

Who could believe
Such a thing could happen
Miracles of Miracles
Arms a'wavin' n' toes a'tappin.

Oh... let me tell you
Why I'm so joyful;
The Lord's blessed me and
His mercy makes my bells
To ding-a-ling-a-ling.

Jesus is real... really here. He's
The Living Bread from Heaven.
Eat His Body, drink His Blood, He
In you and you really in Him.

Becoming more like Jesus, following Him
All the way... living His Gospel like an
Apostle today, sharing the faith
And the reward of Heavenly Grace.

Why not start a New Way...
A New Life... Begin Today!

AN UNFORGETTABLE MASS

Throughout the 1960's I attended the
Summer studies at Notre Dame University.
There were many priests and each morning
I would serve mass at one of the many side
Altars set up all over the Sacred Heart Church.
I will never forget this one mass.

The priest was a humble, simple man. He
Offered the Holy Sacrifice with profound
Intensity and devotion, and handled the
Eucharist With the greatest reverence. It
Appeared as if the veil of faith was removed
And he was actually witnessing the Passion,
Death and Resurrection of Christ.

This common, ordinary and low keyed priest,
Without any emotion or theatrics, manifested a
Depth of holiness that one would relate to a soul
Who ascended to a high degree of union with God.

The Catholic Church's criteria in regard to
Spiritual matters is very wise, prudent, cautious
And discerning because she is the guardian of
Truth and the faith. From the Word of God she
Uses the criteria:

"You will know them by their deeds." Matthew 7:16

Later, I got to know Father. He was undergoing a
Veritable Crucifixion with heroic virtue, forgiveness,
Kindness and supreme charity. His deep humility was
Crowned with an extraordinary Christ-like love for the
One who was causing him so much suffering.

By their fruits you will know them...

AN UNFORGETABLE MASS!

THE SUN

Behold the image in the sky.
A gift from God Most High.

Burning brightly piercing through.
Radiant joy making hearts anew.

Bestowing life, visible parable of
The amazing sun... Merciful Father,
You gave us heaven's gift, Your
Son, the All Holy One.

The Living Bread... so ignored and
Neglected, no reason why... The sun,
Nature's image of the Heavenly Bread.

The Lamb of God, hung on the tree of
The Cross, clothed in purple, a gift for
You... of His very life, to transform you
Into the fiery, burning, melting sun.

Oh, come and merrily rejoice in the hidden
Eucharistic Son. The goodness of the
Lamb of God's victorious battle won.

Let us offer him praise, adoration and
Thanksgiving.

"Then the saints will shine like the sun in their Father's house." Matthew 13:43

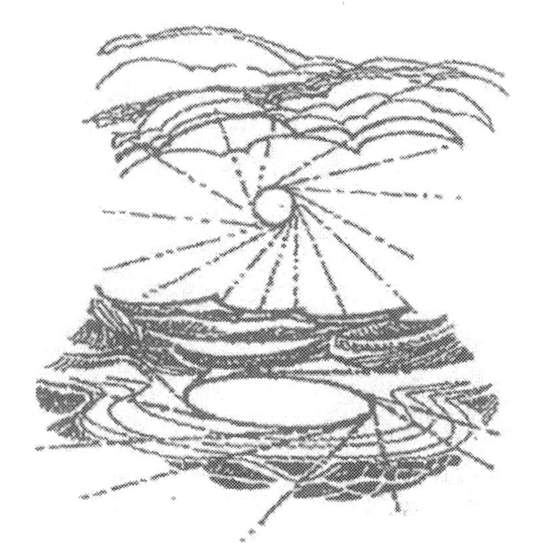

God our Loving Father in His infinite wisdom has created the universe to teach us about the spiritual world of His grace (gift) and His love (life).

God gives us the astounding daily teaching that the Sun in the sky reminds us with joy that it is radiating there to tell us... JESUS IS... TRULY IN THE HOLY EUCHARIST

MARY AND JOSEPH

St. Paul said, *"I beg you, then, be imitators of me."* 1 Cor. 4:16

God has given a gift to us all for imitation,
Mary and Joseph of Nazareth. The Holy and Blessed
Virgin Mary and her faithful spouse, the great St. Joseph,
The just one, humble and kind, the pillar of faith.

Both precious and devout souls lived totally for God,
Manifested in Jesus. Who could begin to describe their
Life together? Their home in Nazareth was truly heaven
On earth, the life of Love, Peace and Joy. It was rooted
In living the Word of God and seeking only to please the
Father and to do His will.

O the beauty of their humility and simplicity of life,
Though poor, yet rich in the treasures of virtues,
Selfless, and living for one another... all in a spirit
Of joy, radiating peace, flooding the earth, gifting
The ages. All was cleanliness, beauty and order.

Jesus comes to dwell with us in His Eucharistic
Presence so we too can experience what the real
Life is all about. The eternal life that is our future
In which eye has not seen nor has ear heard the
Wonderful things God has in store for us all.

They glorified God and gave us an example that one
With faith and simplicity can live a life like theirs.

Ordinary in appearance but truly lived with an
Extraordinary love in a happiness that comes
From living life to the full when you live for Jesus
Who is with us now and present in the Sacrament
Of the Holy Eucharist.

MARY + JOSEPH

*"I bud forth delights like the vine,
my blossoms become fruit fair and
rich.* Sirach 24:17

PLAIN OL' FOOT WASHERS

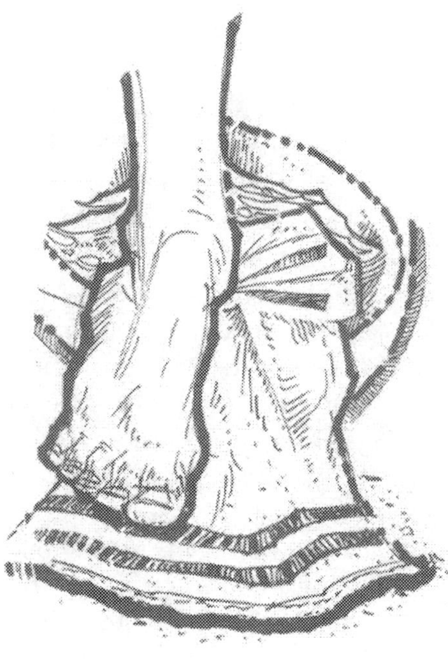

Teacher, Master, Lord am I... I have given you an example
Of what you should be... just Plain Ol' Foot Washers.

Leave behind the endless talk and talk of all that's going on
And stop... in silence remain. Reflect... pray a lot to be
Immersed in My Word. Begin... start now... and do it all.

Reflect on this mystery. The highlight culminated in the
Fulfillment and realization of God's Eternal Passover Meal.

Its fulfillment was the Un-Bloody Sacrifice, the changing of
The bread and wine into the Body and Blood of the
Lamb of God.

The washing of the feet is a symbolic preparation to receive
The gift of the Eucharist. The purpose and fruit of the Sacrificial
Living Bread from Heaven is to receive Jesus who comes to live
In us and we in Him.

It is also about becoming one with others (Communion) in
Unity and Love manifested by humble service, genuine deeds
And caring for one another.

Washing the feet on Holy Thursday is a powerful tradition.
Hopefully, some day in the future may it be used a little more
Frequently in the liturgy. It is a powerful mystery. It is the
Receiving of grace to grow in charity and the imitation of Christ.
Think it over. Become genuine. What resolutions can I make
To imitate Christ's example in serving other? Our Eucharistic
Savior Lord could well say to each one of us...

"No one can out do Me, but with delight, simply try.
It goes without saying; this world could use a few more
plain Ol' Foot Washers."

"What I just did was to give you an example: as I have done, so you must do."
John 13:15

YOU ARE ALL LOVE

All wondrous beauty
O Mother Mary,
Virgin Mother of
The Church, model
Of faith and our
Mother too.

You are the mirror
Of God's perfection
And image of His
Love so true.

The most beautiful
Of all His wonderful
Creation, you who...

"...are the glory of Jerusalem,
the surpassing joy of Israel,
you are the splendid boast
of our people." Judith 15:9

You are all love. A fountain
Of Joy. The first adorer with
Joseph and the shepherds.

"Most blessed are you among
women and blessed is the fruit
of your womb." Luke 1:42

Mother of God, with you in
Glowing adoration we too
Want to adore Jesus in the
Holy Eucharist, and thank our
Father, the God of all Creation,

The Wonderful Giver of all
That is good.

"Mary sacrificed all to God; she
needed Him alone. From this day
forward, I shall follow her example:
The Lord alone will be my portion."
St. Bernadette

IT IS ALL LOVE

Her name was Clare, his Francis… both of Assisi.
Their love was pure, their love was deep. He was
Older, she so young.

But oh the beauty of their love was a fountain flowing
From the charity of God. Not like the world's obsession
With sex and all the disordered fruits blindly pursued.

They loved Christ above everything. They showed us true
Love by way of the Gospel. The way of the Lord, completely
Dying to self, a joyful life of love, wonder and praise.

A tale of friendship that was true, good and holy,
That far exceeds and surpasses the shallow self-seeking lust
And pleasure that the world extols.

Genuine faithful love is one of sacrifice and living
For the other. It is walking together hand in hand with eyes on
The Lord and in the keeping of all His commandments and
Gospel teachings.

With the exquisite kindness, courtesy, respect, dignity and
Mutual caring and sharing that reflects the wisdom, light,
Peace and joy that makes all love and friendship become
Like a paradise on earth.

Francis, the imitator of Christ, bore Jesus' five wounds on his body.
Clare, with faith and trust, held the monstrance of our Eucharistic
Lord before the invading army of the Saracens, who were about to
Storm her convent, but then departed.

We are all made to love and be loved. What was the secret of
Francis and Clare?

TO LIVE IS CHRIST AND LIFE IS LOVE.

WHOM MY HEART LOVES

Love is the mystery of all mysteries. Who can understand
Or comprehend its depths in a bottomless and unending,
Fascination beyond measure.

God who is love itself, has put this wondrous treasure,
A gift of fire that sears, burns and flashes to a flaming pitch.
It enthralls the heart of the beloved.

O how beautiful, savory and relishing a tide of immeasurable
Well-being never experienced as it opens up vistas and
Panoramas of mountain heights of joy.

Scaling, climbing, soaring, running with the speed of a heart
Wounded gazelle upon the terrifying rocks and crags, the
Precipices involved in love's adventures.

All this entails and climaxes in incredible joy and deep
Longing to be united into one. The preparatory plan of the
Almighty to acquaint one with what love is all about.

Earthly love is only a shadow, a faint image to prepare us
For the journey's end of all that is in store for us... the very
Origin and source of love that is in the Sacred Heart of our
God in the Eucharist whom our heart loves.

He who abides in the Holy Eucharist is the only one who can
Fully satisfy our longing for ultimate love. As St. Augustine said,

"<u>Our hearts were made for you O Lord and they will never
Rest until they rest in you</u>."

*"As the Father has loved me, so I have loved you. Live on in my love.
You will live in my love if you keep my commandments even as I have
Kept my Father's commandments, and live in his love. All this I tell
You that my joy may be yours and your joy may be complete. This is
My commandment: love one another as I have loved you. There is no
Greater love than this: to lay down one's life for one's friend."*
John 15:9-13

JOSEPH'S LOVE

When they talked to Joseph
And the subject of his Bride,
The Blessed Virgin Mary
Would enter the conversation.
It would be like turning on the
Lights of the evening stars.

Or like the beauty of peaceful
Views in quiet winding wooded
Streams, splashing delightful sprays
Glistening on the sunlit mountains
With bird songs gracing the air.

Golden rimmed forests reflect his
Humble, gentle and faithful love for
His exquisitely Beautiful Bride, the
Blessed Virgin Mary; the pure and
Immaculate Mother of God who gave
Birth by the Holy Spirit, and that Body
And Blood would be given and shared
With everyone in the Holy Eucharist.

Mary and Joseph's life of faith, silence
And gentle simplicity drew them to an
Intimate union with the Lamb of God.
Now extended and shared with all of us
When we offer and partake in the Divine
Liturgy, receiving the Bread of Angels as
We soar to the seraphic heights of purity
And holiness in joyful love for all eternity.

Mary is the symbol of the Church, the Mystical
Body of Christ. Joseph is our Great Protector.
With Mary and Joseph we sing with hearts of
Gratitude and joy:

"How beautiful you are, how pleasing, my love, my delight."
Songs of Songs 7:7

THE MANGER

"And this will be a sign for you: you will find a baby wrapped in swaddling clothes and lying in a manger."
Luke 2:12

"The ox knows its owner and the donkey its master's crib; but Israel does not know, my people does not understand."
Isaiah 1:3

"And they went with haste and found Mary and Joseph, and the baby lying in the manger."
Luke 2:16

Of all places on earth, why did God not choose the
Most sumptuous palace or the most incredible beauty
Of nature in keeping with His Divine Majesty
And awesome Holiness?

God Himself would come to save His people and
Give them New Life. First as a child, later as a shepherd.

A manger?

The feeding trough for animals?

In God's impenetrable wisdom and unimaginable
Merciful love... He would make Himself Eucharistic
Bread for the Life of the World and in His humble way,

Inviting you to come... eat... and be one with Him.

MY TRINITY TREE

It's so very special.
There's nothing like it.
Majestic in dignity
Unlike any other
In its threefold
Towering trinity
Like form, rising
To the endless
Expanse of infinity.

Its soft light green
Moss and its
Unusual separated
Rhythmic bark
Diversified, yet
One in unity,
Has always enthralled
Jacinta and elicits
A breath-taking
Awe and wonder.

Within it, my beloved
Jacinta's creative
Imagination conjures
The image of the
Trinitarian branches
Projecting the
Crucified savior.

Beneath the Leaves of Grace,
Sharing His Blood, His Love
And His Eucharistic Life.

My wife, Jacinta, was fascinated with this
Unusual tree outside the center at Marianna.
She ask me if I would write a poem on it.

GOD'S TRADEMARK

God's Trademark? The five wounds proving His love for you.

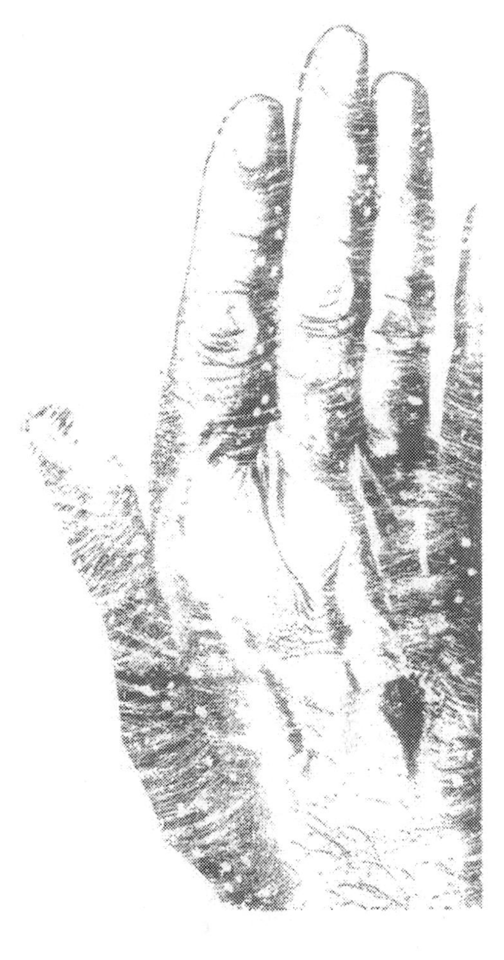

Also...
God's indelible trademarks are Beauty, Cleanliness and Order. Whether in persons, places or things, they reveal the depths within. The lack of such on highways, streets, yards or buildings evokes mankind's failing stewardship. Havoc wrought from the results of original sin and what is going on in today's world. Is it not revealing what is going on in the hearts and lives of us all?

One's appearance and dress, or the houses we live in, the cars we drive, the desks, rooms, drawers and closets, reveals within us our disordered lives reaping joyless faces and at times producing listlessness, even depression.

It is a prophetic cry and plea to change our hearts, attitudes and dethrone our blinded selves. Behold how we claim our inability, weakness and indifference where excellence is lacking. Do we not unconsciously desire perfection, happiness and well-being, yet how often do we sadly reap sorrow, pain and discouragement.

Yet hope springs eternally. Pope John Paul II the Great left us a legacy of the dignity of man, encouraging us to

"Cross the Threshold of Hope."

When we eat the Bread of Heaven, the Bread of Life...we cross over to the green pastures where we are made Clean, Pure and Radiant, cleansed from sin and strife to know that Peace the world cannot give.

Peace... the trademark of the Holy Eucharist.

"Behold, I have graven you on the palms of my hands." Isaiah 49:16

NEW LIFE

"In the beginning was the Word and the Word was with God and the Word was God. He was in the beginning with God; all things were made through him, and without him was made nothing that has been made. In him was life, and the life was the light of men. The light shines in the darkness; and the darkness has not overcome it." John 1:1-5

God called Abraham and chose Israel, and his descendents, our Jewish brothers and sisters to receive His Holy Word and fulfill His promise of restoring the Supernatural Life lost by our first parents, Adam and Eve.

The Old Testament foretold that the promised Messiah would come Himself to shepherd His flock. Jesus is the Resurrection and the Life who came to give all of God's children life... and life more abundantly.

Throughout the ages His voice rings out the Good News of great joy:

"I am the way and the truth and the life; no one comes to the Father, but by me." John 14:6

All life is the incredible gift of God, sacred and precious. Our Creator shares with us His very own supernatural life. We are all made in His image and likeness. Only God and God alone... can give life and take away life.

Jesus is the Bread of Life who came down to give life to the world. He is the Door of the Church and to eternal life. By the Sacrament of Baptism (Greek, *baptizein*, to dip in water) the soul is incorporated into the Church to give us His new life.

"I solemnly assure you, no one can enter into God's kingdom without being begotten of water and spirit." John 3:5

"Truly, truly, I say to you, unless you eat the flesh of the Son of man and drink his blood, you have no life in you; he who eats my flesh and drinks my blood has eternal life, and I will raise him up at the last day. For my flesh is food indeed, and my blood is drink indeed. He who eats my flesh and drinks my blood abides in me, and I in him." John 6:53-56

For the Journey of Life Jesus gives Himself to Us in the Holy Eucharist.

MYSTERIOUS MORNING

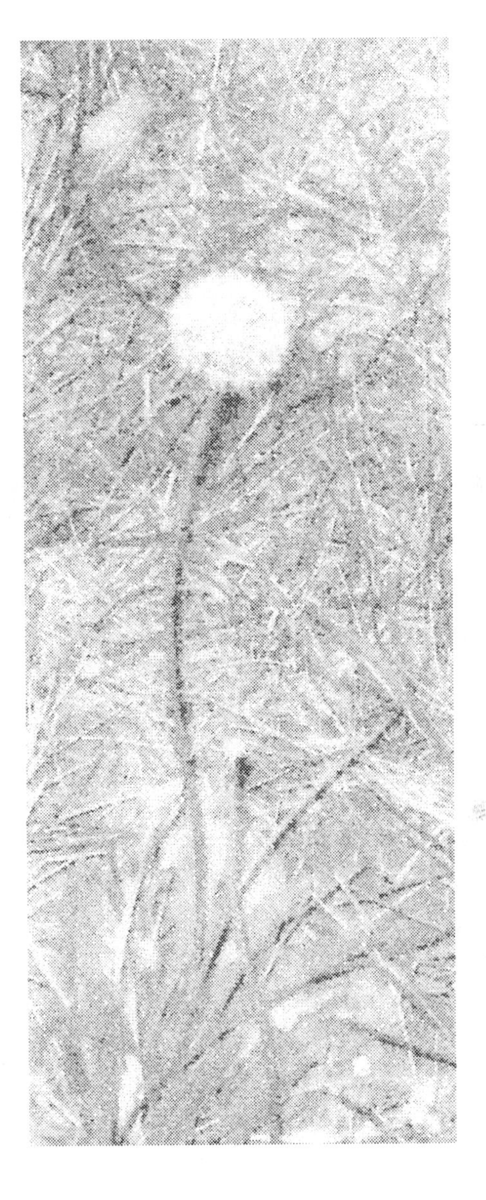

A pensive quiet morning.
The grass in a hushed silence
Beyond the shadowed brush,
Beyond the roadside, beyond
The leafy glen's silent gaze.

A hazy mist obscures the corn
Field covered in fog. It is so
Different, hardly any birds with
Their morning songs to stir
Announcing another day.

Everything is so unusual, enveloped in
A mysterious atmosphere of expectation;
Only the distant hammering of workers
Framing a new house is heard.

The birds in stillness still, as crickets start
Their steady shrilled sounds, seeking,
Piercing, probing as if to discover what
The world's future will bring.

And in the midst of it all is one solitary
Little dandelion giving reassuring hope
Of eternal life, far beyond what this is all
About.

*Do not be afraid when problems, suffering and
Despair are overwhelming. The Holy Spirit,
Our Savior Lord in the Holy Eucharist, our
Lady and St. Joseph will help bring about a
new world and a new life for us all.*

DIVINE MERCY

Jesus I trust in You. You are goodness, humble love and Mercy divine. You are unfathomable grace... a heart on fire. An ocean of unending forgiveness, compassion, sweetest tenderness so far beyond all understanding, so great the mysterious depth of Your unimaginable yearning to draw all souls into the joyful mercy of inexhaustible peace. Taking the greatest sinner in an instant, to make an incredible saint of incomparable radiance beyond all measure, the saving gift of Your Holy Eucharist...
Our Angelic Bread Divine.

"See, I have left My heavenly throne to become united with you. What you see is just a tiny part and already your soul swoons with love. How amazed will your heart be when you see Me in all My glory." No 1810

"But I want to tell you that eternal life must begin already here on earth through Holy Communion. Each Holy Communion makes you more capable of communing with God throughout eternity." No. 1811

Diary, Divine Mercy in My Soul
St. M. Faustina Kowalska
Marians of the Immaculate Conception,
Stockbridge, Massachusetts 01263
Used with permission

Annie Karto, a beautiful Singer and Apostle of Divine Mercy asked me if I could illustrate her song on Divine Mercy. The above sketch is what it looked like and is now in Sr. Faustina's convent in Poland.

I SAW GOD

In the early hour morn, God rose from his slumber… an awakening musical voice stirring His creative Powers to paint a new daily canvas of a jeweled landscape and sky.

Creativity beyond imagination, His sacred gift of infinite beauty with myriad varieties of muted colored delights and enchanting pigment styles in an ever changing artistic mural of awesome living art.

The stars of heaven sing the Glory to God in a concert of light, lifting us up out of ourselves to immerse us in Divine Peace, distilling Faith… enabling us to catch a glimpse Revealing the Author of all Creation.

What a vision of a magnificent gallery

of breath-taking works of art. See the drifting illuminated clouds in all their majestic glory announcing His veiled presence with the sun's rising dawn.

Like the Eucharistic Lamb's Glorious exposition, where in adoration I now rest in the goodness and beauty of our Savior Lord and God… our Sacrificial Mystical Lamb of the Sacred Paschal Rite.

"Trust in the Lord and do good; so you will dwell in the land, and be nourished in safety. Take delight in the Lord and he will give you the desires of your heart."
Psalm 37:3-4

"Divinity is always where one least expects to find it."
Archbishop Fulton J. Sheen

"He has showed you, O man, what is good and what does the Lord require of you but to do justice, and to love kindness, and to walk humbly with your God?"
Micah 6: 8

MY SPIRITUAL DIRECTOR

A stalwart pillar and strong towering oak like

The ocean's depth. As surfing waves, in timeless

Bubbling foam. A rhythmic cadence feeding the

Rock laden shore. Thirsting for the waters of life

In the sparkling, glistening, light… absorbing the

Reflection of wisdom's depth, clarity and soaring

Heights of truth. Ohhh, the radiance of Jesus in

The Eucharist and in the beauty of His Word

Wrapped up in the sagacity of the ages, emanating

Humility. Having washed nature's cocoon, bursting

Forth the Spirit's fruits, gifts and power into the

Sacerdotal mind, heart, spirit and soul of the Lord's

Gift to us all… Our beloved Spiritual Director,

Father Venantius Preske, has a singular love for the

Sacred Scriptures and who gives all the glory to Jesus

In the Holy Eucharist. To the Most High Lord,

God of Love, Father, Son and Holy Spirit. Amen

Poem about my Spiritual Director who is gifted by God and has a profound humility.

JOINED IN ADORATION

"Who is this that comes forth like the dawn, as beautiful as the moon, as resplendent as the sun, as awe-inspiring as bannered troops?... How beautiful you are, how pleasing, my love, my delight!"
The Song of Songs 6:10, 7:7

No beauty can compare, exceeding all pleasure. A feast of delight, praise beyond measure. The bearer of Light, Tabernacle of the Most High.

Adorned with virtue higher than the angels, awesome in sight, purest of all lilies.

Behold the Virgin Mother, humble and kind. Spouse of the Holy Spirit. Joy of heaven. Hope of all the earth.

Ever selfless and caring. Living solely for God and as Mediatrix of all Grace, Advocate and Co-redemptrix, forever bearing in her Immaculate Heart the children of the Lord the Most High.

Sanctified by His Blood, and fed by His glorified Body, the Bread of Heaven.

Together with her, joined in adoration and praise, let us worship Him in the Holy Eucharist and give Glory to her Divine Son.

"How many among the best Catholics never pay a visit of devotion to the Most Blessed Sacrament to speak with Him from the heart, to tell Him their love! They do not love our Lord in the Eucharist because they do not know Him well enough. But in spite of knowing Him and His love and the sacrifices and desires of His Heart, they still do not love Him, What an insult!"
Saint Peter Julian Eymard
THE REAL PRESENCE

Eymard Libray, Vol. I
Cleveland;
Emmanuel Publ, 1938:
PG. 149-150

THE BUTTERFLY

This morning I was making my thanksgiving
After receiving Jesus in the Holy Eucharist.

It happened in the early morning amidst
The beautiful creation of God's great out-
Of-door's Cathedral

A page on the Apostles was being written
When a Butterfly landed on my chest.
It remained there.

I believe it was a message meant for you.

God has a very special mission for You.

IT IS HOLINESS.

That Jesus, our Eucharistic Savior Lord
Wants you to know that He, with the
Father and the Holy Spirit comes to you
In His Holy Word and Sacrament of the
Eucharist to live in you.

You are the Living Tabernacle of God. Your soul
Is made in the reflected image and likeness of God.

The Butterfly is a symbol of the Resurrection and New Life.

"If a man loves me, he will keep my word, and my Father will love him, and we will come to him and make our home with him."

John 14:23

THE APOSTLES

Jesus built His Church on Peter. *"And I tell you, you are Peter, and on this rock I Will build my Church, and the gates of Hades shall not prevail against it."*
Matthew 16:18

Filled with the Holy Spirit, they proclaimed

The Good News of the Gospel…the words

And deeds of the Risen Christ.

TO LIVE IS CHRIST…AND LIFE IS LOVE.

The Holy Eucharist is the Heart and Center of our Church and the Christian life.

The Church is called to evangelize the world
By sharing the joy of Our Risen Savior Lord.

As He called Peter and the Apostles, so He
Now calls you…

**To be a Saint of the Eucharist, and
An Apostle, to give witness to the
Humility and Charity of Christ.**

For all our Catholic and non-Catholic Brothers and Sisters, there are two outstanding books based on Pope Benedict XVI's weekly teachings;

"The Apostles And Their Co-Workers"
(Our Sunday Visitor, Inc.)

"Jesus, the Apostles And The Early Church"
(Ignatius Press).

YOU TOO!

When the Priest at Mass holds up the Eucharist and says:

"This is the Lamb of God; who takes away the sins of the world. Happy are those who are called to his supper." We respond, "Lord I am not worthy to receive you, but only say the word and I shall be healed."

What do we see?...

We see Jesus under the appearance of bread.

The very same Jesus that was in the womb of our Blessed Mother Mary. The very same Jesus that worked with St. Joseph, who preached to the crowds, worked miracles and healed many...

"But blessed are your eyes because they see and blest are your ears because they hear. I assure you, many a prophet and many a saint longed to see what you see but did not see it, to hear what you hear but did not hear it.
Matthew 13:16, 17

You too can be with the same Jesus as He was then and is now. He is Radiant in Beauty and Glory in the Holy Eucharist. In Scripture you too can listen to Him, the living Word of God as He speaks directly to you.

"You are the salt of the earth... You are the light of the world... come to me ...and learn from me, for I am gentle and humble of heart ...come after me and I will make you fishers of men."
Matthew 5:13, 14; 11:29, 4:19

Jesus wants saints; Jesus needs saints. Another St. Francis of Assisi? Another Mother Teresa? Another St. Theresa of Lisieux? Another Cure of Ars?

<u>No, No! He wants you to be the person you are.</u>

Saints are like us. They too failed every day. Ups and downs, fits and starts. The difference is that they kept going by doing good. They always trusted in Jesus, and never gave up. He makes up for all that we lack. The more impossible one is the better Saint material they are. Because we know then it is the Lord who can do it, and is doing it. He will always astound us. For with God...nothing is impossible.

YOUR SPIRITUAL ORDERS

When the Lord commanded
Moses, He gave the Israelites
The orders what to do and how
To conquer the land.

Our Lord now commands you
To change your heart and all
Your ways.

He is about to give you a New
Life…to make all things new,
To share with you His very life.

It matters not, how weak or
Sinful you are. He will give you grace
And all the help you will ever need.

Return to the sacramental waters
Of Reconciliation. Receive strength
Through the Mass, the Breaking of
The Bread. Live a New Life in the Holy
Eucharist and the Sacraments.

You will taste the joy of being
Free if you remove the obstacles.
Then the gifts and fruits of the
Holy Spirit will work powerfully
In you and through you.

"Today if you should hear His voice, harden not your hearts." Hebrews 4:7

"In the Eucharist Our Lord is the model of our interior life. There His life is chiefly hidden, silent, loving and sacrificed. Such also must our life be.

"He loves to give Himself to us in Holy Communion… He desires sanctuaries where He will be exposed for veneration, be visited, loved and consoled. Have we the same desire?"

SPIRITUAL DIRECTORY, The Eucharist
Page 41,42
Fr. John Leo Dehon, S.C.J. (Founder)

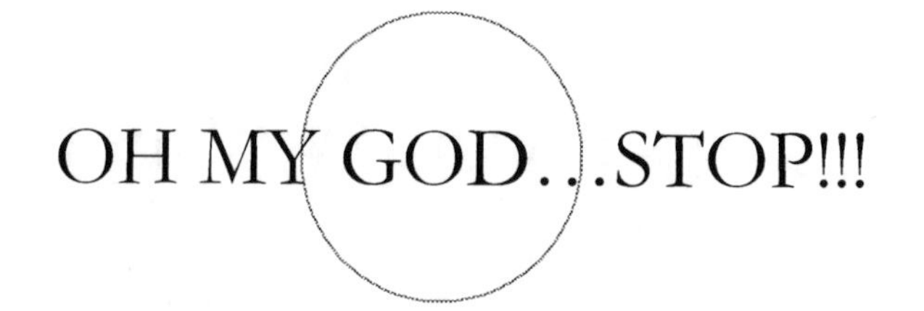

OH MY GOD…STOP!!!

Hey…stop, stop, stop! ...STOP!!...PLEASE!!!

He is truly innocent. He never did anything wrong, Believe me… please … for heaven's sake. Look, they're tearing His flesh To shreds! Make them stop…OH…MAKE THEM STOP!!!

You're giving him a blood bath. It's splattering all over. He has never hurt anyone… He utters no cry, like a Lamb going to be slaughtered.

My God, He's no criminal… only meek, mild and humble of heart. Stop whipping Him. You cannot even recognize Him anymore. So hideous, like a worm and no man, despised by the people.

They are plucking His beard, raining down blows and covering Him with vile spitting. Roaring and raving like lions. They are bringing Him down to the dust of death.

His heart has become like wax melting away in His breast. Betrayed, denied and deserted… all alone is He. Oh God, my God, why have you forsaken Him? Far from words is His cry.

Oh… won't anyone do something? They are mad, they are crazy. They are beasts, not even the animals are that ferocious and cruel. How terrible He is suffering, yet utters no cries. Only sadness.

No human being could take or survive all this. Please … Please! Stop… I confess. He is taking my place, it is me… I'm the one. I am the guilty one. He has taken all my sins and is laying down His life for me… for me… Do you hear? Not Him. Whip me. Don't you know who He is? Last night, after washing our feet,

He took bread and wine,
Changing them into the
Eucharist, and His
Precious Blood, giving us
His Body and Blood…
To set us free…
Free at last,
Now…
One are we…
We are one…

FREE AT LAST

MOTHER TERESA/MAHATMA GANDHI

Pope John Paul II canonized 483 saints and beatified 1,342 men and women. More than all the Popes since the Council of Trent. When Mother Teresa was asked how one became a saint, and replied, "Die now, the Pope's canonizing everybody."

When Archbishop Daniel Buechlein was in Memphis, Tn. he invited Mother Teresa to bring her Sisters to help the poor. They came. Mother insisted that the air conditioning, rugs, etc. be removed as her Sisters were not to live better than the poor they served.

Jacinta and I would bring our Pilgrim Virgin Ministry to Mother Teresa's Covent in Memphis, Tennessee. With the Pilgrim Virgin statue and the Gospel message we would pray the Rosary with Sister Suma Rani and her Sisters who were always joyful and humble with beautiful, childlike simplicity. With infectious liveliness the Sisters faithfully wore their religious habits and veils. When people met them they were inspired and grateful, seeing them as truly Brides of Christ.

Mother Teresa instilled a tremendous love for Jesus in the Holy Eucharist and had in all her houses, above every tabernacle next to the crucifix, the inscription: *"I Thirst."* Jesus is the center of their life and work which they passionately live for. India declared her Co-Patroness of India along with Mahatma Gandhi as the Father and Mother of their Country. He said that *"if he believed Jesus was in the Eucharist that he would crawl on his knees into the Church and lie prostrate before him."*

The Sermon on the Mount was an inspiration to Gandhi. He looked upon Christ as the ideal representation of non-violence and the law of love. He was a man of great courage, humility and peace. His life was an inspiration for the ages. He demonstrated the awesome power of prayer can accomplish the impossible. He lived the ascetical life of the Gospel that humbles us who should be living it in deed and truth.

Both Mother Teresa and Mahatma Gandhi were single-minded persons of peace. They understood the power of prayer, fasting and virtue. When traveling, Mother Teresa would inform the Superiors that she would clean all the toilets. Rising at 4:30 a.m., she would begin the day with the Lord in prayer.
Her faith and love for her Eucharistic Jesus inspired her to serve Him in *"the poorest of the poor,"* throughout the world. She completely died to self and lived to serve everyone in whom she saw Christ. She said,

"The time you spend in the presence of the Blessed Sacrament is your greatest time spent on earth."

Mother Teresa had a love and respect for everyone knowing we are all children of God. Regardless of race, color, creed or nationality, she cared for and humbly served everyone in need. **Like Blessed Mother Teresa and Mahatma Gandhi, may we too help make it a better world through goodness, kindness, helpfulness and love for the poor and those in need.**

NATURE'S BEAUTIFUL BENEDICTION

n this early fresh
Spring morning, it is a
Paradise unfolding...

God the Divine Artist has created all things. Everything in creation tells us about Him for which we offer continual praise and thanksgiving through Christ who is the image and glory of the Father.

Completely in awe and wonder... my
Heart is enthralled, my eyes aglow
Enchanted with nature's glorious
Benediction. Surrounding beauty,
Inexpressible for words while gazing
At nature's gifted bouquets bestowed
Upon us by the Lord.

Oh look! See the unending variety of
Colors, shapes, forms and continuous
Messages of sparkling protestations
Of His infinite love...

Slowly descending dew...glistening
Gems from the trees above, while
Beams of light slowly awaken through
The foliaged sky as a little bird joyfully
Warbles God's good morning greetings.

Wake up my children... My Eucharistic Sun is
Rising above the horizon bringing to all the world
The blessing of dawn's grace filled dew
In the early morning splendor of the glorious
Easter Resurrection Light.

THE HOLY FAMILY

Blessed Holy Family, no more beautiful
sight on earth.

The Word became Flesh and dwelt
among us with the Holy, Immaculate
One and her great stalwart oak tree,
St. Joseph.

They were The Holy Family of
Sanctified grace and peaceful joy.
For it is, and ever shall be…but
so many experience it not…
as you can see.

Oh, lift up your eyes, seek the beyond,
where dwells the Most High, the Family
of Three… now in mystery wrought as
the warmth reaches out, embracing all,
giving new life and joy supreme.

For the Trinity…Father, Son And Holy Spirit,
transforms us through the Bread from Heaven,
all families on earth into the one glorious family
of the Kingdom of God in everlasting peace and
unity, world without end. Amen.

If God used one poor, lonely little man called Noah
to end the evil on earth, the symbolic instrument
of Christ's redemptive sacrifice to make all things
new through the sanctifying waters of grace.

Then what is to prevent God from using you to
Help the world and the one family of God, to
Become His Holy Family once more?...and to
See the beautiful sight of a new rainbow in the
Heavens over the earth made holy by our
Eucharistic Savior Lord.

GIFT OF FIRE

"I don't want to set the world on fire" was a popular Song when I was growing up. In Greek mythology, Prometheus brought the gift of fire to humanity. However, man would not want to literally set the world On fire, yet wars and evil seem to speak otherwise.

In the mystery of the Incarnation, God's love Culminated in Love's supreme fulfillment of His Mercy, forgiveness and the restoration of man's Paradise lost and the Divine Life.

"I come to cast fire upon the earth, and would that it were already kindled." Luke 12:49

This is the true gift of fire to humanity. Indeed The world has been set on fire. The invisible, all Powerful, eternal, ever blazing fires of love Through Word and Sacrament burning in the Heart of Christ, who is the manifestation of our Merciful God… our Father Almighty

In the Holy Sacrifice of the Mass and in the Holy Eucharist, the Divine Fire consumes and Transforms all of creation and the heart of man Into the burning flames of charity elevated by Grace into the very life and love of God.

OUR GOD IS A CONSUMING FIRE.

Our Eucharistic Heart of Jesus is the radiant Light of God's glory.

'Know thyself' is by far the wisdom of the ages. Faith, trust, the Mass and Adoration of the Holy Eucharist is the ultimate of all.

JOHN PAUL II / BENEDICT XVI

Pope John Paul II the Great
Pope Benedict XVI the humble Sage
Rock of Peter / Proclaimer Paul
Guardians of the Faith and Truth of all
John Paul the Transcendent one
Benedict the Enlightened one
John Paul the Dignity of Man
Benedict the Magnifier of the Word

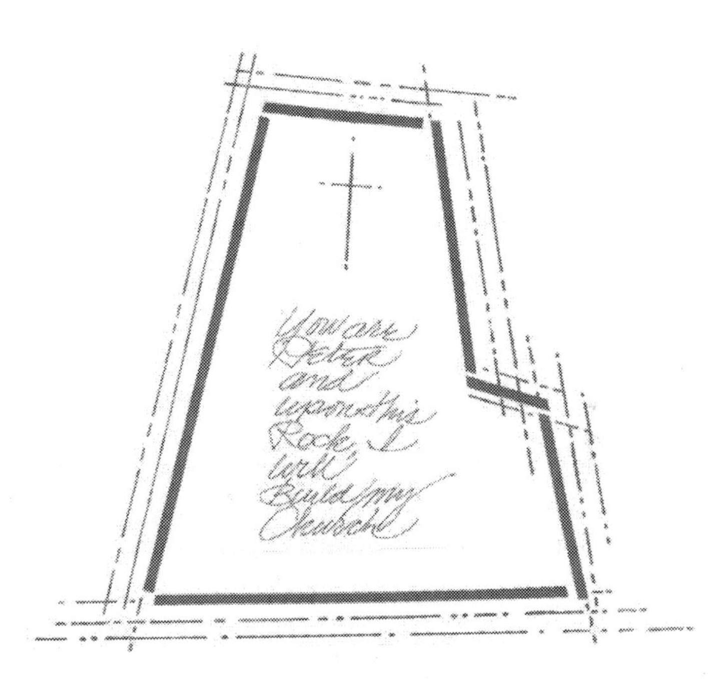

John Paul the Crucified one
Benedict the Prophetic One
Light for the World
Salt of the Earth
John Paul Philosopher of Man
Benedict Wisdom of the Ages

John Paul Forgiveness and Peace for All
Benedict Christian Unity, Father of All
John Paul the wall came tumbling down
Benedict connecting the dry bones
John Paul Vibrant with life
Benedict the Teacher of the Way
John Paul the Exalted
Benedict the Profound

John Paul II...

Popes of the Eucharist...
Stalwart Gibraltar's

Benedict XVI

Twin gifts of God for the Church,
The World and for You
Motivators for justice,
Goodness and brotherly love.
Beloved Sons of Mary...
Successors of Peter
Beacons of Light
Followers of Christ's Way

A LOOK OF LOVE

When the cock crowed, Jesus turned
And looked at Peter.

O look of love, Look at me and in Thy mercy please
wash me clean in Thy blood bedewed.

O look of love, Look not at my sins, for You will only
find a feeble treasure of deeds or virtue
true.

O look of love, For I am nothing of the nothingness
and all I have is a yearning trust and
hope in You.

O look of love, You and You alone, is all I have.
If only I could live life over again.

O look of love, Never, never would I ever want to hurt
You again my kind, gentle and beloved
Savior Lord.

O look of love, Your tears are mingled in anticipation of
the beautiful waters of Baptismal and
Reconciliation graces.

O look of love, Now forgiven by my compassionate
Jesus, made immaculately clean...
pure and incredibly new.

O look of love, You are my happiness, my life and my love.

O look of love, Oh how I Love You... Love You...
ever Loving... Loving You...

My Loving Looking Lord.

Now present in the Holy Eucharist, I fall on bended
knee to worship You with grateful joy, humbly
returning Your...

Beautiful Look of Love.

*"I love you, O Lord, my strength.
The Lord is my rock, and my
fortress and my deliverer, my God
my rock, in whom I take refuge,
my shield, and horn of my salvation,
my stronghold.*

*"For who is God, but the Lord?
And who is a rock, except our
God? The God who girded me
with strength and made my way safe."*

Psalm 18:1-2; 31-32

STONE COLD

Cold as a stone like
A bump on the log.
Heart of granite
Mind in a fog.

Distracted thoughts like
Dripping rain
No light to see
Only memories of pain.

Blackened, dead embers,
Smokeless fire vanishing,
Always night; never near.

A time of darkness in
Unbearable silence, all
Quiet and quieter still.

It all seems so eerie, one
Sided and no one there.
No sound nor murmur
Not even a word.

Despite this bitter darkness
A dawning night aglow…
Faith… Gilbraltar's Rock.
It is so.

Deliberate, surest path
Climbing the elevated
Mountain of God.
In his Holy Word
Behind the curtained veil,
His Eucharistic glory…
The dark night never so bright.

CHAPLET OF THE EUCHARIST

AT THE CRUCIFIX...

The Apostles' Creed
I believe in God, the Father
Almighty, creator of heaven
and earth.

I believe in Jesus Christ,
his only Son our Lord.
He was conceived by the
power of the Holy Spirit
and born of the Virgin Mary.

He suffered under Pontius Pilate,
was crucified, died and was buried.
He descended to the dead.

On the third day he rose again.
He ascended into heaven and is
seated at the right hand of the
Father.

He will come again to judge the
living and the dead.

I believe in the Holy Spirit,
the holy catholic Church
the communion of saints,
the forgiveness of sins,
the resurrection of the body
and the life everlasting. Amen.

The first bead:
Our Father, who art in heaven, hallowed be Thy name; thy kingdom come; thy will be done on earth as it is in heaven. Give us this day our daily bread; and forgive us our trespasses as we forgive those who trespass against us; and lead us not into temptation, but deliver us from evil. Amen.

On the three beads:
Come Holy Spirit, come by the means of the powerful intercession of the Immaculate Heart of Mary, your well beloved spouse and the great St. Joseph

On the fifth bead:
We believe you are truly present
In the Holy Eucharist, the
Sacrament of Love

Before each decade:
O Sacrament Most Holy, O Sacrament Divine, All Praise and All Thanksgiving be Every moment Thine.

On the ten beads of each decade:
Eucharistic Heart of Jesus grant that we may love You more and more.

After each decade:
Holy Mary, Beautiful Mother of God, pray that we may all be one in our Savior Lord.

Prayer at the end of the chaplet:
Glory be to God the Father,
Glory be to God the Son,
Glory be to God the Holy Spirit,
Holy Three in One. Amen

WITHIN

Deep down within
Beyond the minds
Examining the depths
Of reality and
The penetration
Of truth immerging
From the unknowing
Of understanding

One with deep
Emotion opens
Wide the arms
Of welcome to
The indwelling

Presence of the

Holy One

The exalted
One who calls
Himself the
Way, the Truth
And the Life

Forsaking all
Shedding all
To embrace
Simplicity...

And no longer
Live... save in
His Word and
In his Bread.

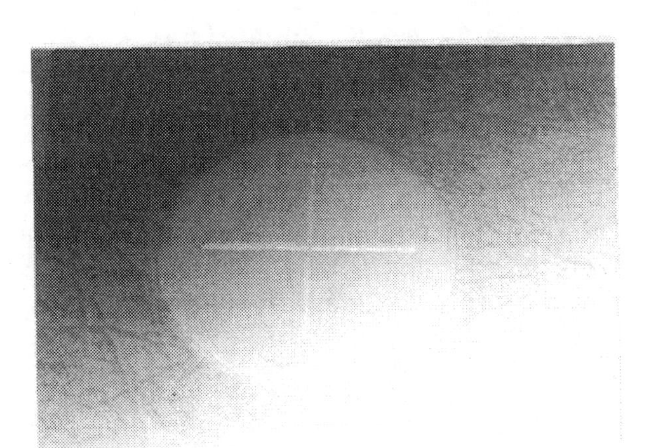

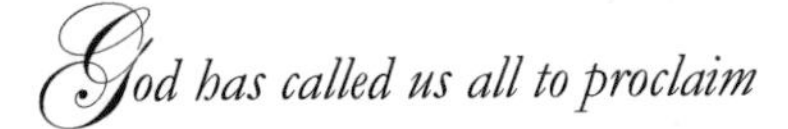

God has called us all to proclaim the Good News. Jesus has suffered, died and is risen from the dead. He is giving Himself to us in the Holy Eucharist.

I have responded with poetry, art and prose.

And you?

He is calling you to respond by your holiness of life and to radiate the joy of the Lord who will always stand by you.

Jesus gives you His grace and gifts along with the talents He has given you; that you may or may not be aware of... or have not used.

HOPE FOR ALL IN PRISONS

(LET THEM THANK THE LORD FOR HIS STEADFAST MERCY AND LOVE)

O Saint Dismas, what a mess you were. A born loser; such a promising future and you blew it. You had it all but made wrong choices and followed the path of darkness. You who were made in the image and likeness of God... You who had dignity and were made by your Creator to be His beloved child. To lose everything, even your entire divine inheritance. You became a criminal... and like Adam in Paradise lost it all.

You were on the Cross... crucified, suffering, hurting, regretting, yet despairing and ending up like this. When lo and behold, you were given the Most Loving and Holy Mother ever born. The suffering, sorrowing Mother of the Crucified One who was praying for you Dismas. **FOR YOU**... for every single son and daughter hurting, angry, despairing and living in a vale of tears or imprisoned behind bars; or the prison of addiction or the most horrible of all... sin.

Your Mother Mary prays and intercedes for you... offering her sorrows and sufferings with Her Son's Death to the Father on behalf of all her new born sons and daughters.

Dismas, the prayer of the most holy, purest and beautiful of all women, prayed and interceded with her Divine Son, the Lamb of God. He offered His life and blood to wash every single soul no matter how guilty or sinful. They become new born sons and daughters. He died to make everyone pure and holy... totally new. He wants to have them in His everlasting kingdom of love, peace and joy.

Of all that could be said of the Holy Eucharist, it is central in God's plan of salvation. Like Mary's Magnificat, the "Eucharist means first of all *thanksgiving* and praising God through, in and with Jesus in the memorial of His sacrifice giving glory to the Father
"...for all that God has made good, beautiful and just in creation and in humanity." Catholic Catechism, No. 1359

"Lead me out of prison that I may give thanks to your name." Psalm 142:8

"See, upon the palms of my hands I have written your name." Psalm 49:16

"Truly I say to you, today you will be with me in paradise." Luke 23:43

To be free... free at last. See, Mother I make them all completely New.

"Some sat in darkness and in gloom, prisoners in affliction and in irons, for they had rebelled against the words of God, and spurned the counsel of the Most High... Then they cried to the Lord in their trouble, and he delivered them from their distress; he brought them out of darkness and gloom and broke their bonds asunder. Let them thank the Lord for his steadfast love, for his wonderful works to the sons of men!" Psalm 107:10-11, 13-15

THE NEW QUEEN ESTHER

The Mother of God was symbolized by Queen Esther in the Old Testament. She interceded for her people with King Ahasuerus. He granted her plea to save her people.

There is hopelessness in our world with an ever increasing deterioration of all that is "*honest, pure, admirable, decent, virtuous or worthy of praise.*" Philippians 4:8

It is increasingly flooded by egoism, hatred, violence, wars, impurity, relativism, materialism, pleasure, greed and gross injustice.

Our Lady is powerfully interceding for the Church and the whole world...

"I will call to mind the deeds of the Lord; yes, I will remember your wonders of old. I will meditate on all your work, and muse on your mighty deeds. Your way, O God, is holy. What god is great like our God? You are the God who works wonders, who has manifested your might among the peoples. With your arm you redeemed your people, the sons of Jacob and Joseph. Psalm 77:11-15

IT WILL ONLY BE ACCOMPLISHED THROUGH CHRIST AND THE GOSPEL!

The renewal of an individual, the Church and the world will originate through the Holy Eucharist in union with Mary and is realized through the transforming power of the Eucharist, culminating into the very love of the Heart of Christ.

MY SON, MY SON…

I die death's dying
Day of the Lord, His hour has come
O innocent Lamb of God

My Son, My Son…

The vicious lions roar, totally depraved
They lash out, mean, ugly and spiteful
O sorrowful sea of evil's cruelty

My Son, My Son…

Welled-up fountain in bitter tears
Jaws of hell fanning flames of fire
In His blood all sin is redeemed

My Son, My Son…

Tortured, brutalized, all agonized
In utter distress, darkness covers the land
Only groaning covers His broken heart

My Son, My Son…

Cruel lashes, thorns and searing nails
Ever suffering beyond all imagination
Messiah sacrificed in blood's libation

My Son, My Son…

Out of death comes life
Body sacrificed, sublimated
In the Cross of Eucharistic love

My Son, My Son…

Thorn crowned, stricken and crucified
Divine seed dying on the Tree of Life
Love's triumph and reign of eternal life

MY GOD, MY GOD… OH MY GOD, MY LOVE

THE SECOND PENTECOST

O Spirit on high
Eternal flames
Of burning love
Love of the Father
Love of the Son
Burning love of
The Holy Spirit
According to the
Riches of the
Father and for
His glory, come
Descend, come
Upon your One
Holy, Catholic,
Apostolic Church
And all your
Children. Come
O come to transform
Each one and all.
Come over the face
Of the earth
Come flame
Of the Father
And the Eucharistic
Heart of the Son,
Come mightily in
The roar of your
Flame and Breadth.

Proposed sketch for oil painting on Pentecost

"And that Christ may dwell in your hearts through faith; that you being rooted and grounded in love, may have the power to comprehend with all the saints what is the breadth and length and height and depth, and to know the love of Christ which surpasses knowledge, that you may be filled with the fullness of God." Ephesians 3:17-19

THE MORNING STAR

In the silent darkness of the night looking
Out my window the early morning hour
Veils all...

'Tis black.

Save for the window reflection of the library
Lined bookshelves not even the stately oaks
Are visible at all...

'Tis black.

Yet above in the dark velvet sky the glowing
Sight of a glimmering star, wisdom's pathway,
The guiding luminous light to behold.

Tis dawn.

In a hopeless, loveless troubled world
Beyond what man can change or even turn
Around... Yet Hope springs eternal.

The pure radiating light, precursor of the dawn
Is the beautiful Virgin's icon...

Tis the Morning Star.

Guiding her children on their Way of the Cross.

In faith's journey unseen with emerging hope in
Her Eucharistic Son's Easter radiating Light.
Announcing the gathering together of the
The Eternal Eucharistic Wedding Banquet.

Silence is the language of God. Jesus speaks to us In the Holy Eucharist through silence. Wisdom Enters through love, silence and detachment.

Do not pay attention to what people say and do Around you. To obtain the highest union with God, center your heart and life on Christ, the Radiant Star of Joyful Love.

MOM AND THE HOLY EUCHARIST

My father, Julius, was a great man. He was a good father and very talented. I want to share some memories of my mother, Nicolina Prosperino Di Cresce. She went by the name of "Nellie." Mom was unique and special. A beautiful person so greatly loved by everyone. She had a big heart and an attractive personality that endeared her to everyone.

Mom was a listener and possessed the gift of sympathizing, encouraging and consoling. She was most generous. Mother was no shrinking violet. She spoke her mind and was direct, open and honest. She spoke plainly. You knew exactly where she stood. Mom had a nice balance and possessed wisdom and common sense. She treated everyone with respect and graceful manners. I can still picture her beautiful smile wreathed with infectious laughter. She lifted up low spirits with the sage advice that, *"Yes, life can be tough, but life can also be beautiful."*

Our mother had a simple and deep faith. She had a pure, kind and generous heart that was manifested by her deeds and action. The warm atmosphere of our home was like Grand Central Station with a continuous stream of visitors. Mrs. Tutott, our neighbor across the street, said *"Land sakes alive, I don't know how your mother can get anything done with all those visitors."* Mom always served coffee and refreshments.
Mom was devoted to the Blessed Virgin Mary and her rosary. She influenced me in having a great love for the Mother of Our Lord. As a young boy she would take me along to the Tuesday evening devotions of Our Lady of Perpetual Help. How I loved Benediction of the Blessed Sacrament. It was special.

Benediction made a profound impression on me. A love was instilled for our Savior Lord in the Holy Eucharist. I will always be grateful for my mother.

Our Lord told Gabrielle Bossis in my favorite spiritual book, "He and I", that *"Every woman is a part of my Mother Mary."* How true. The most beautiful love on earth is the love He has put in every woman's heart. God has endowed them with selfless giving and gentle care. They sacrifice themselves to bring happiness and well-being to others. We were blessed with wonderful Parents and treasure those memorable years we had with them.

Gratefully, Mom believed God gave everyone life at the moment of conception. With His Eucharistic love and mercy God gives us His gift of eternal life. No matter how difficult, hopeless or impossible the situation you must always live in total hope.
With man it may be impossible but with God everything is possible. Remember, God loves you deeply, intimately… and yes, most faithfully!

MUSIC

Music is the awesome voice of
The spirit. Whence comes the
Vibrations awakening the strings
Of the Heart?

Elevating the mind from earthly
Matters that bind, spiraling upward
Into the universal language of the
True invisible reality…

Beautiful music, Life in the Spirit,
The soul in communion with the
Mesmerizing strains intoxicating
Hearts in the ever awakening joys,
Satiated longings of all fulfillment.

Overflowing desires in the dancing
Waters of peaceful harmonies,
Delightful nuances, surprising melodies,
Resonating, echoing refrains that draw
The soul into the sunlight of eternal glory.

For how else to penetrate the Divine
Mystery of the Holy Eucharist?

Saved by faith with beautiful music in
The ever-rising praises and the deep
Heart felt songs of worship, engendering
Humble thanksgiving and adoration of
Our God in His Eucharistic love and glory.

"Sing for joy, O heavens, and exult, O earth; break forth, O mountains, into singing! For the Lord has comforted his people, and will have compassion on his afflicted. Isaiah 49:13

Music is the universal language that can
Unite all peoples to lift up their hearts to
All that is true, beautiful, honest, pure,
Virtuous and worthy of praise.

"I will sing to the Lord all my life;
I will sing praise to my God while
I live. Pleasing to him be my theme;
I will be glad in the Lord… Bless
The Lord, O my soul! Alelluia.
Psalm 104: 33, 34-35

"I am convinced that music… really is the universal language of beauty which can bring together all people of good will on earth and get them to lift their gaze on high and open themselves to the Absolute Good and Beauty whose ultimate source is God himself."

Pope Benedict XVI at the Vatican
Concert for his 80th Birthday

DEACON EUGENE/HOLY EUCHARIST

When Deacon Gene was bringing Holy Communion to a Parishioner he fell, seriously wounded, and suffered greatly For six years. He was confined to his bed and not able to Walk again. He truly led a crucified life. He and his wife, JoAnn, gave witness of deep faith and a profound Christ-like Love in their practice of heroic virtue.

In critical condition at the end he was asked if he wanted to stay Or go to heaven. "Heaven," he replied and then peacefully went Home to his eternal reward. Around 1500 persons paid their Respect and farewells at the wake and Mass. Grown men cried. Many shared their memories of a Deacon immensely loved who Made an impact on their lives.

Gene and JoAnn's family also gave a moving witness of their Genuine love for one another. They are a close family. His Funeral Mass was an incredible celebration of new life. People Had never experienced such an inspiring and joyful funeral liturgy.

There were 25 Priests, Deacons and two choirs. A homily and eulogy were brilliantly given by The two Monsignors, both of whom he served, and the past and present Pastors. The joyful Atmosphere continued on as the parish community had a big celebration in the Church hall of St. Joan of Arc. The amazing amount of food brought by the parishioners for the celebration was a Generosity matching Gene's generous well-known giving. This is a reflection of what the Eucharist is all about. Worship, thanksgiving, sacrifice, unity and the Christian fruit of a genuine Love for one's neighbor in deed and truth.

Deacon Gene had a faithful love for his Master in the Holy Eucharist. He loved his vocation and Ministry. He went all out in serving others. It was his life and keen desire to live the life of the Gospel. His care for everyone made quite an impact. Gene's reputation will long be Remembered as a faithful, holy follower of Jesus.

My gentle, kind and humble brother, Deacon Eugene Edward Di Cresce, loved to give gifts. He Stored up a large supply so he could generously give them to others. His reputation made it a Kind of reality that every day was Christmas for a Christian.

God's greatest gift to us, each one and all... is His Son, Jesus, in the Holy Eucharist. This was Gene's life and love, along with his deep love for his beautiful Bride, JoAnn. Now he is home With his Eucharistic Lord in glory. Home, at last. Helping to prepare and excitedly waiting for The day of the Lord when we will all finally be gathered together in the Eternal Eucharistic Wedding Banquet in the Kingdome of God.

A NOCTURNAL VOICE

In the purple silence
Of the night,
Adoring You
In Your hidden
Eucharistic
Presence
In the quiet early
Dawn before all
Creation is awakened
A nocturnal voice
Is heard...
A lonely somber
Sound...
As the distant
Freight train heads
Unseen in its
Journey winding
Along its melancholy
Way
To be for
Us all...
A kind of icon
Of our earthly
Pilgrimage
Passing through
A dark night
Of tears into
The uncharted
Waters of the
Eternal delightful
Joys of the
Risen
Eucharistic
Sun.

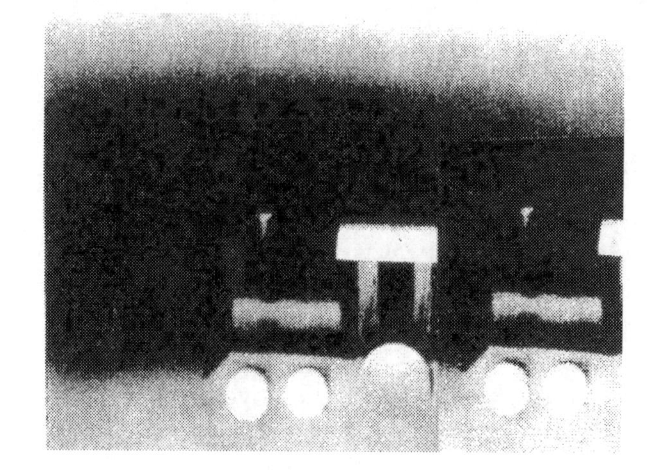

The greatest treasure on earth
the Pearl of Great Price is
Jesus in the Holy Eucharist...
the Sacrament of Love.

REPARATION

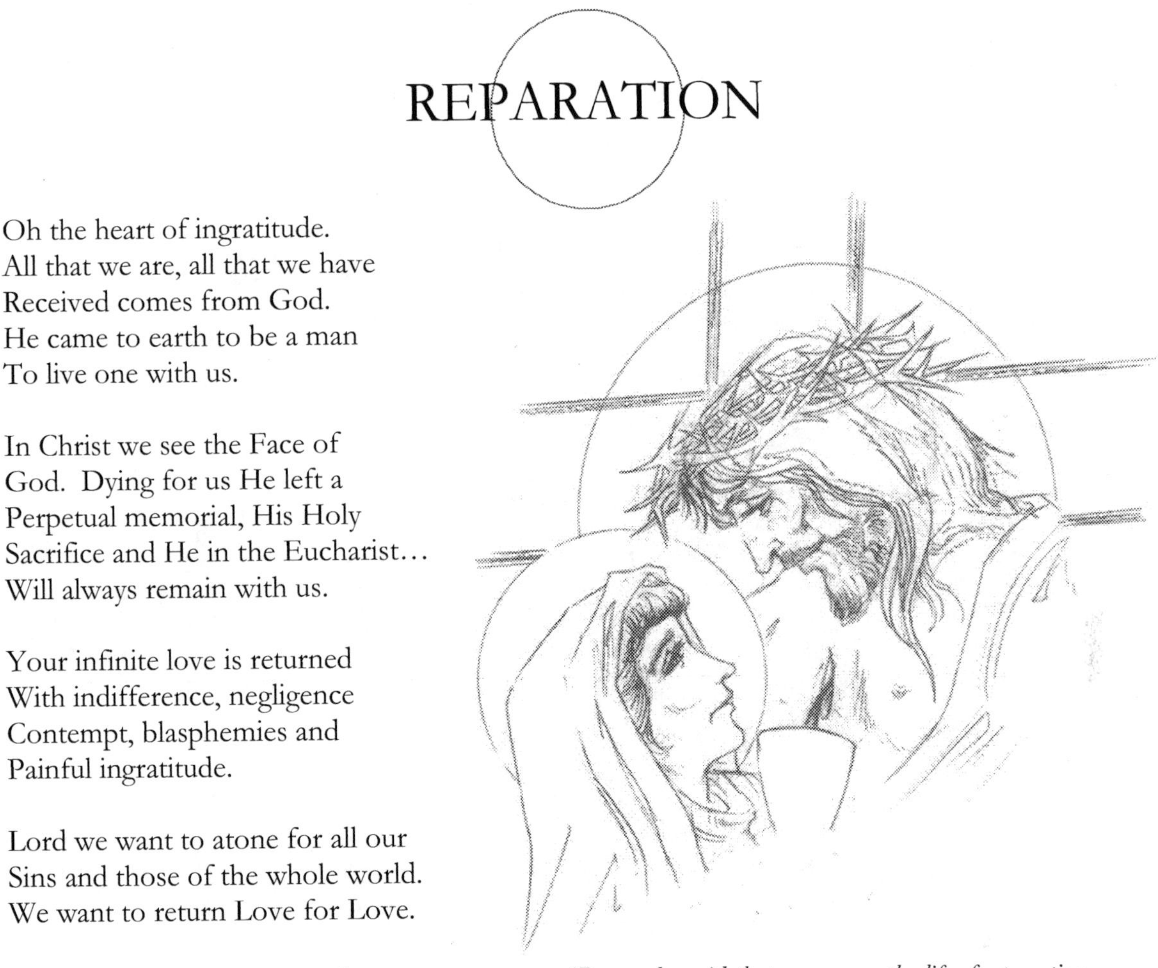

Oh the heart of ingratitude.
All that we are, all that we have
Received comes from God.
He came to earth to be a man
To live one with us.

In Christ we see the Face of
God. Dying for us He left a
Perpetual memorial, His Holy
Sacrifice and He in the Eucharist...
Will always remain with us.

Your infinite love is returned
With indifference, negligence
Contempt, blasphemies and
Painful ingratitude.

Lord we want to atone for all our
Sins and those of the whole world.
We want to return Love for Love.

We long to console You and
Make up for all those souls
Who wound Your Heart and will
Have nothing to do with You or
Defy You in the breaking of Your
Commandments and teachings.

Jesus, with Your Beautiful Mother
Mary we appeal to your infinite
Love and mercy. Set our hearts
Aflame so we may restore all hearts
To Your peaceful reign
By faithfully responding to
Your resounding cry...

"I THIRST"

"It may be said that never was the life of reparation more wanted than it is in our days, for never was God so publicly outraged, so fearlessly blasphemed. Never has the ruin of souls been so complete, for the faith of the people is sapped to its foundations. Never has scandal been so widespread, for it has become national, nor so disastrous, for it attacks even childhood, our last hope. Now, more than ever, then, has our Lord need of souls who seriously and generously make reparation, and aid Him in atoning for these outrages against God, in saving souls from ruin, and in repairing these awful scandals."

LOVE PEACE AND JOY
by Fr. Andre Prevot, SCJ
Third Edition, Pg. 106
Tan Books and Publishers
Used with Permission

WORD OF GOD

St Jerome: "Ignorance of Scriptures
Is ignorance of Christ."

Lord, help us to understand the Scriptures,
The living and powerful word of God.
Like the gentle rain that comes down to
The earth...watering the land, giving birth
To the flowering fields with harvests of
Golden grains.

The Word of the Lord is for all nations, all
Races, all peoples... everyone is in our One
True Family of God.

O Word of God in Your wisdom and love
Divine You descended to earth resting on
A manger of straw.

O Little Child, nestled in Your Mother's arms
Drinking her pure Virginal milk... the Holy One
The Immaculate One... in tears we are bathed in
Adoring Adoration.

The Word became Flesh and dwelt among us and
Oh... so humbly we fall on bended knees in the
Presence of the Light and Love Divine.

"...blest are they who hear the word of God and keep it."
Luke 11:28

Confessing our poor love, our blinded, material,
Self-centered idol self, give us Your holy word...
Yourself, in the Holy Eucharist, the Gift of God.
For there is nothing more I would rather have,
Nothing more I need or want... than to be one
With You.

I AM ALL YOURS.

*Sacred Tradition and Sacred Scripture
Form the deposit of the Word of God
Handed down through the succession
Of the Apostles and entrusted to the
Teaching of the Church whose authority
Comes from Jesus Christ.*

*"For as the rain and the snow come down
from heaven and do not return there but
water the earth, making it bring forth
and sprout, giving seed to the sower and
bread to the eater, so shall my word be
that goes forth from my mouth; it shall
not return to me empty, but it shall
accomplish that which I intend, and
prosper in the thing for which I sent it.*
Isaiah 55:10-11

BEAUTY EVER REVEALING

When I see beauty Lord, I see You.
You are beauty itself. In Your glorious
Creation, the overflowing fountain of
Your awesome beauty emanating from
Your heart O God, You who are
Rapturously in love with us all.

Gifting us with Your sun, moon and
Galaxy of stars. The unending variety of
Flowers, fields of golden wheat, the snow
Capped mountains, streams and valleys.

The delicacy of snow flakes, the glistening
Intricacies of spider webs and the unending
Procession of animals, birds, fishes, sights,
Sounds, aromas, rain and changing seasons.

See the glorious sunrises and sunsets.
Spellbinding in their exquisite pastel hues.
The beauty and uniqueness of each and
Every person with their immortal souls
Radiant in Your very image and likeness.

But that which surpasses them all,

Oh... the beauty of the beloved
Master... dwelling in the

Holy Eucharist.

How I long for the day to see His adorable face.

"When shall I go and behold the face of God?" Psalm. 42:3

YOU A SAINT OF THE EUCHARIST?

Of course. Why not? Never say, "Oh no, not me."
Jesus commands you: *"It is God's will that you grow in holiness."*
1 Thessalonians 4:3

In plain words Jesus says that you are to be holy as I am holy.

Yooooouuu? Ohhhhh Yeeeeesss!

To be holy is simply to be one with Jesus.

Another Christ. You cannot do it, but with God all things are possible. Just trust.

This is all God's work. You are his masterpiece Our Lady, Mediatrix of all Grace and St. Joseph Will help you to walk with Jesus.

"The time is fulfilled, the kingdom of God is at Hand, repent, and believe in the gospel."
Mark 1: 15

"The first step in holiness is having only love In your heart." Ronda Chervin

"Just do little things with great love."
Mother Teresa

"Being Holy means living in profound communication with the God of Joy."
Pope John Paul II

Is he really calling you? Yes, He is calling you Now. Each one of us is So unique and no one else is like you. You may never Have thought about it. You are very special in God's heart. The Saints are the movers and the shakers; the ones who Change history and make It a better world.
Yes you... God has a Definite plan for you...
it is holiness!

"The saints, as we said, are the true reformers. Now I want to express this in an even more radical way, only from the saints, only from God does true revolution come, the definitive way to change the world."
Pope Benedict XVI, 10th World Youth Day in Cologne, Germany

Dorothy Day wrote a book on St. Therese of Lisieux, because she was the saint of "the little way:. It is about fidelity and trust in bringing love of God into the routine of daily life. Doing little things for love of God. Fully aware of living in a time of great Evil throughout the world, she believed The only success of combating it was Sanctity.

O COME LITTLE CHILDREN

O come little children, come and see
Your humble Savior a little baby
Softly crying with tears of joy.

He lies on the manger hay with arms
Wide open to hug and hold you in
God's embrace who is meek and gentle
And Ohhh, so little... just for you.

Knowing that you might be afraid,
Trembling at His Majestic power
That could scare you to death.

Yet His only desire is to have
You smile, laugh and lovingly
Embrace Him... and warmly
Rest on His Sacred Heart.

His tiny fingers touch your lips
To be still... to say no more...
For He is yearning and cannot
Wait to lay on His Cross on Calvary
Just because He loves you so much.

To take away all your sins and
Sorrow and by becoming lowly,
Humble Bread so you will be
One with Him... truly one
In Everlasting...
Love, Peace and Joy.

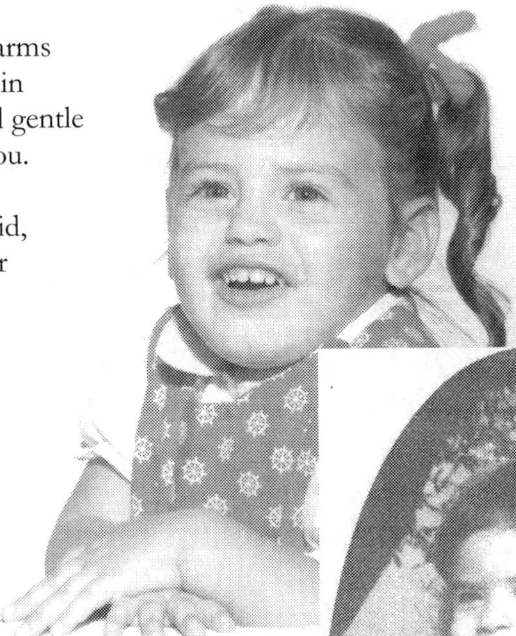

HIGHLY RECOMMENDED READING

ONLY ONE BOOK...THE BIBLE... God speaks
To you in The Old and New Testaments, the Gospels
And the Epistles. It is not just a book, it is the Living
Word of God. The Holy Spirit will give us power
And the remembrance of all that Jesus said and did. It
Is the love and inspiration of God, the outpouring of
The Father's gift to strengthen and guide us. The
Bible inspired by God is entrusted to the Church so we
May grow in faith and live a Eucharistic life of Holiness.

"Your word is a lamp to my feet and a light to my path." Ps. 119:105

The Holy Spirit's intimate breath of Divine Life is
Warm, simple and profound giving us the power
Of making us a New Creation to bear much fruit.
The smile of God, the awesome Word of God, the
Second Person of the Blessed Trinity became the
God-man to dwell among us.

First, by becoming a little baby. Then the Son of Man
Among men who is the living Bread of God from Heaven.
He who has all power in Heaven and on Earth gives
Himself to us so we may live in the very life and love
Of the Holy Trinity and share the joys of Eternal Life,
Forever.

"Through him all things came into being, and apart from him nothing came to be. Whatever came to be in him, found life, life for the light of men. The light shines on in the darkness, a darkness that did not overcome it."
John 1:3-5

Read and live the Word of God every day. The Word of God comes to
Us in the Holy Eucharist and speaks to us in the scriptures. He will change
Our lives to make us all new. With the Beautiful Mother of God and with
All mankind we sing...

"Strip away all that is filthy, every vicious excess. Humbly welcome the word that has taken root in you, with its power to save you. Act on this word. If all you do is listen to it, you are deceiving yourselves." James 1:21-22

DO NOT LOOK

DO NOT LOOK AT ANYONE ELSE.

Do not look at other nations...
All of us can strike our breasts.

Do not look at leaders and our
Politicians... we are no better.

Do not look at the rich with scorn, both
They and we are poor beyond measure.

Do not look at movie stars and the famous
They fail in one way and we in another.

Do not look at the specks in your neighbor's
Eyes and not the logs in your own.

Do not look at others and all that's going on,
For the answer and the solution is to look in
The mirror, and with Pogo exclaim:

"We have met the enemy and they is us!"

**Go to adoration, look and adore Jesus in the
Holy Eucharist... No greater love has he than...
To lay down one's life for one's friends.**

Scrutinize
Self-knowledge
Remove your blindness
New understanding
New beginning
Become Christ-like

If each and every one of us becomes what God wants
Us to be, to live by His wisdom and commandments,
Then... Oh then... everything will begin to fall into place.

And gradually our world... our lives... will know
Peace and the well-being of everyone on earth.

RECEIVE THE POWER

Pope Benedict XVI, during the
Australian World Youth Day
Said, *"You will receive power when
The Holy Spirit has come upon you and
You will be my witnesses."*

The power of divinity overcomes evil.
His power is descending on the world.
His power is descending on you.

You have read this book about
God's immense love for you.
His becoming simple, humble
Bread to be one with you

Think about it...
Pray about it...
What to do about it?...

Pray and listen...
God speaks to you
In gentle whispers

May Jesus Savior Lord
In the Holy Eucharist
Through the power of
The Holy Spirit in you...

Become like a fountain of
Living overflowing waters
And ignite your soul with the
Grace of strong enduring hope.

RECEIVE THE POWER!

Pope Benedict XVI said Divine Mercy is
The power against the evil of the world.

SWEET MYSTERIES OF LIFE

The power of God's
Word is mighty. It
Also comes to
Us through
The Sacraments.

Sweet Mysteries of life.
The Sacrament of Penance
Is the restoration of
Divine Life wherein
You become a new
Person in Christ.

We are called to die daily,
To turn away from self
And be like a flower
Turning to the radiating
Sunlight.

Changing one's heart...
Doing penance... for the
Kingdom of God is here
And now. Nearer than
You are to yourself.

In receiving the sweet mystery
Of the Sacrament of the
Holy Eucharist, you enter into
The very fire of God's Love.

To radiate the living presence
Of God dwelling in you and...
Life in the unity of God's family.

Ahhh...wonderful, awesome powers!

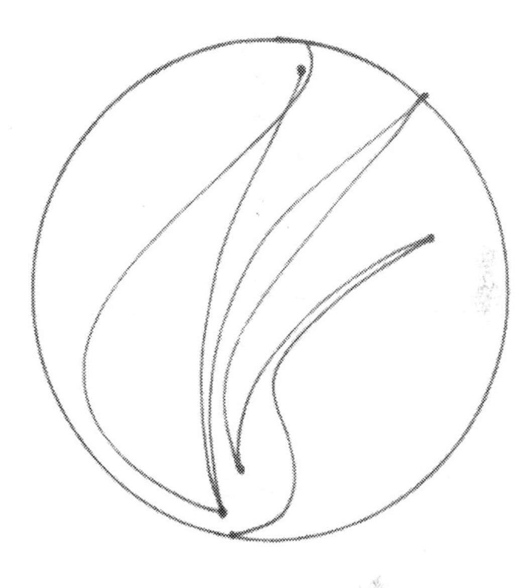

The Sacrament of Holy Eucharist
and the Sacrament of Penance
give supernatural grace that is
powerful and can accomplish far
more than your human efforts to
change your ways if you cooperate
with the Grace of God.

FRIENDSHIP

"A faithful friend is a steady shelter: he that has found one has found a treasure. There is nothing so precious as a faithful friend, and no scales can measure his excellence. A faithful friend is an elixir of life; and those who fear the Lord will find him. Whoever fears the Lord directs his friendship aright, for as he is, so is his neighbor also." Sirach 6:14-17

A treasure of wealth,
Riches beyond measure.
A joy unending
The celebration of life.
A depth penetrating
Of marvels to behold.
The inner warmth
Radiating fire aglow.
A peace affirming
In an awesome garden
Of beauty enthralled.
When storm and rain
Darken the landscape,
A true faithful friend
Is a warm sunny day
In the fresh beauty
Of early springtime.
Present in the Eucharist
Is Jesus who is Love….
Wrapped in gentle kindness
And genuine caring with an
Outpouring of affection
Because you are deeply
Loved by the most faithful
Of any friend you could

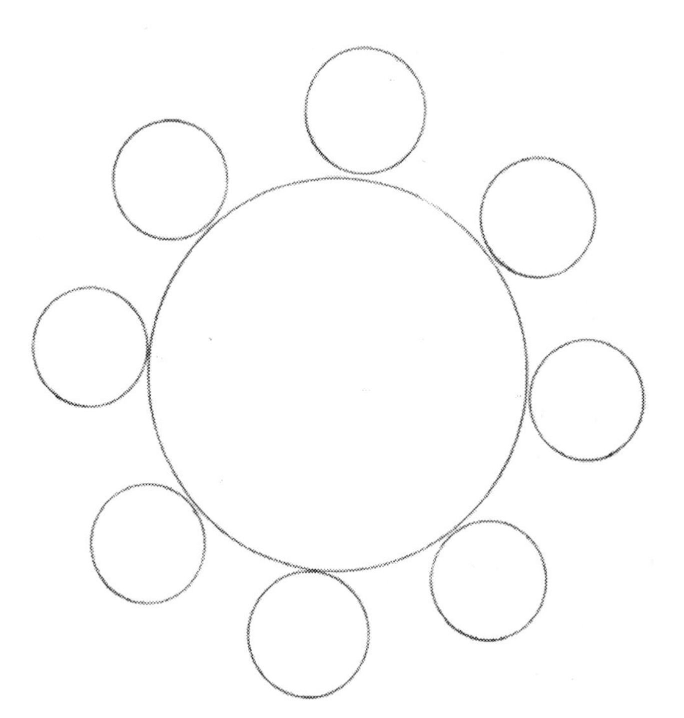

Ever… ever, have.

MY BELOVED LORD JESUS

O radiant fire of joyful Love
My sweetest, Jesus, beloved Lord
O light of light, shining bright
Eternal Word of the Most High God
Spotless Lamb, purest white of
Heaven's Sacred Eternal Banquet.

Adorable Bread of Angelic hosts
Magnificent Song of Song's beloved
King of Kings, Lord of Lords…
Powerful, fearsome, awesome might.
Incomparable meekness, O humble heart
The Good Shepherd, Our all Holy Yahweh.

A rapturous gaze of the hidden, Divine
Lord, Oh exultation of the soul's delight.
Fresh living waters flowing from the
Sacrificial Victim… the angelic, paschal
Bread, of grace, love and communion.

Impenetrable, veiled mystery and
Consuming fire… Sacrament of Holy Unity.
The beautiful Virgin's child, radiating
An incomparable, glorious beauty and
Peace… Jeshua, the well beloved Son,
The Father's supreme joyful delight.

Ardent lover… all lovers' adoration
O oceanic mercy's fountained depth
Who could ever fathom the mystery
Of God's stupendous humility and care.

**You are my Joy, my Life, my Fire, and my All…
O my beloved Jesus, my Eucharistic Savior Lord.**

GARDEN OF DELIGHT

In the morning like
The garden of long ago,
When you walked and talked
And shared Your word.

Now, in another garden of
Delight, with bird songs
Weaving through the sun
Spotted shadows.

The dancing pine trees
Swaying in delectable
Delight, in the mist of
Dawn's early morning air.

In revering field's
Rippling, surfing waves
Accompanying the ocean's roar
Of the Holy Spirit's presence.

All in a concert of praise
And adoration of my newly
Resurrected Savior Lord...
Jesus in the Sacred Bread.

Now transformed and talking
In the silent stillness of faith,
Lifting me up to the very heights
In a melting heat of flames.

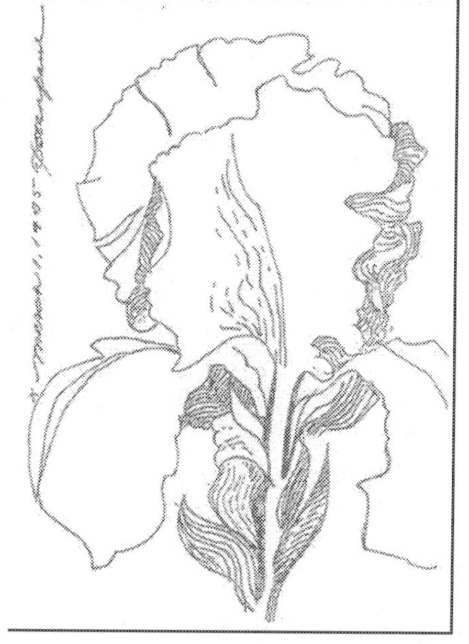

Thanksgiving after Communion in God's Great Outdoor Cathedral. What I call it when outside in God's wonderful creation.

THE LAMB OF GOD

For this He came… for this
He longed to accomplish
The culmination of His
Divine wisdom, the climax
Of Creation. The revealing
Of His love exceeding the
Boundaries of understanding.
Both of the angelic world
And the mind of mankind.

The Lamb of God in His
Incredible Supper wherein
The iconic Passover is melted
Into the New Testament of
Love… the fulfillment
And longing of the ages…

When this singular mystery
Becomes the sum total
Of all that is and all there
Is to be, embracing…

Transforming… all evil
And suffering in the
Breaking Of the Bread
That is offered simultaneously
With every Mass, that is the
One Eternal Sacrifice of Christ's
Redemptive offering that takes
Away all sins through the pure,
Merciful Love of God in
Bestowing Forgiveness…

For all God's children and
In the sharing of the Most
Divine life of
The Holy Trinity…
Father, Son and Holy Spirit.

HOW CAN I KEEP FROM SINGING

"Who are you?"
"I am Jesus, Son of the Most High.
"Are You really there in the Holy Eucharist?"
"Yes."
"You mean all this time since you left the earth?"
"Yes."
"Why?"

"Did I not promise you, "Behold I am with you Always, to the close of the age." Matthew 38:20
"As God aren't You everywhere?"
"Yes, but I want to share with you my Divine Life."
"Isn't that hard to do?"
"Love makes it easy."
"Cool, I'll have to tell everyone about You."
"Please do. I will be most grateful."
"What do You do all day in the tabernacle?"
"You ask many questions."
"O.K. Jesus, then You ask me a question."

"Who then are you?"
"I am Peter Paul."
"Peter Paul."
"Jesus."
"Peter Paul."
"Jesus."

"Peter Paul I love you" ... *"Jesus I love you"*...
"Peter Paul I love you" ... *"Jesus I love you"*...

"Jesus, we're sounding like two little chickadees chirping back and forth."
"We are no longer two; you and I are now really one."

"No storm can shake my inmost calm while to that rock I'm clinging.
Since love is Lord of heaven and earth, how can I keep from singing?
Quaker Hymn, Robert Lowry, 1826-1899 Public Domain

TRANSFORMATION

"The light shines in the darkness." John 1:5

When you come to
Know Jesus in the
Holy Eucharist
Your blindness will
Be Transformed into
His Light...
His Word
His Truth
His Mercy
His Peace
His Beauty
His Power
His Wisdom
His Kindness
His Gentleness
His Goodness
His Humility
His Simplicity
His Joy
His Compassion
His Majesty
Beyond all Desires
Fame, Materialism
Money, Sex, Power
Knowledge, Intelligence
Enjoyment and pleasure.

To be transformed into...

His Infinite Happiness
His Infinite Holiness
His Infinite Love
His Infinite Creativity
His Divine Radiance...

Jesus invented the Eucharist so you would be totally one in Him.

WHERE JESUS IS, THERE IS JOY

"Where Jesus is... There is Joy
There is Peace
There is Love

And that is why He made himself."
THE BREAD OF LIFE

To be our life of love and joy.
No one else can give what He
Gives, and He is there all the time.
We have only to realize that.

"Jesus has said very clearly:
I am the love to be loved
I am the life to be lived
I am the joy to be shared
I am the Bread to be eaten
I am the Blood to be drunk
I am the Truth to be told
I am the Light to be lit
I am the Peace to be given.

JESUS IS EVERYTHING"

Blessed Mother Teresa of Calcutta

"Words To Live By... Mother Teresa"
Pg. 12-13

Glory to God in the highest,
and peace to his people on earth.
Lord God, heavenly King,
almighty God and Father,
we worship you, we give you thanks
we praise you for your glory.
Lord Jesus Christ, only Son of the Father,
Lord God, Lamb of God,
you take away the sin of the world:
have mercy on us;
you are seated at the right hand of the Father;
receive our prayer.
for you alone are the Holy One
you alone are the Lord,
you alone are the Most High,
Jesus Christ,
with the Holy Spirit,
in the glory of God the Father. Amen

Hymn of praise when the One, Eternal,
Sacrifice of Christ is offered to the Father
in the Holy Sacrifice of the Mass

TRIPLE POWER

In our times we were
Pleased with the gifts
In the persons of...

Pope John Paul II
Pope Benedict XVI

Lovers of the Holy Eucharist

Defenders of the Faith,
Proclaimers of the "Sacred
Tradition and Sacred
Scripture that form
One sacred deposit of
The Word of God."
(Vat. II "Dei Verbum" No 10)

We are blessed with
The TRIPLE POWER of...

Sacred Scripture
Vatican II Documents
Catechism of the Catholic Church

These wonderful gifts of God
Are the necessary means to
Renew ourselves
Under the guidance of
The Holy Spirit,

"...so that we may be found increasingly faithful to the Gospel of Christ."
Vatican II, Council Opening Message to Humanity

"Under the guidance of the Holy Spirit, we wish to inquire how we ought to renew ourselves, so that we may be found increasingly faithful to the gospel of Christ."

Vatican II, Council Opening Message to Humanity

Purchase them...Read them...
Study them...To know your faith...
Live them...Pray and discern them

So you may give witness To Christ and His Love in deed and truth to the entire world.

ST. PETER AND ST. PAUL

The cock crowed twice. Peter failed,
And three times denied Our Lord.

Paul was the raging enemy of Christ
And the fiercest persecutor of the Church.

Both of whom were the most unlikely
Choices that God could ever make.

For great is Your mercy and mysterious
Your ways to build Your Church and
Guide Your flock.

How encouraging.

Oh Lord, You fill our hearts with joy
As we honor Your great Apostles,
Peter, the Jewish Rock of our Faith,
Paul, the Apostle to the Gentiles.

Through their labors, witness, and
Martyrdoms, they sacrificed all for
Love and unity of the One, Holy,
Catholic and Apostolic Church,
The Mystical Body of Christ.

Following in their footsteps may we
Too, with courage and zeal, be the
Eucharistic and Evangelizing Apostles
Of today.

To carry the cross and bring the message
Of the gospel by the holiness of our lives
To gather the harvest of souls for the Lamb
Of God and the Glory of His Kingdom.

*With St. Peter and St. Paul we want to
Place Jesus Christ in the center of our
Lives through communion with Him
And His word.*

AT THE LAST SUPPER

When our Savior Lord instituted
The Eucharistic Sacrifice of
His Body and Blood, He in
His divinity saw you and as
The Lamb of God He took
Away all your sins by His
Precious Blood to make you
Completely new and to be
One with Him.

You can say, "He did it for
Me out of His infinite
Loving kindness and mercy."

OUR LADY OF GUADALUPE

Juan Diego, a humble Aztec Indian was Chosen by God to be our Beautiful Lady's Messenger to North, Central and South America and to the entire world.

Like the poor shepherds of Bethlehem He heard the Heavenly music on a cold Winter day and was instructed by our Beautiful Mother of God to gather the Flowers on top of the hill now a paradise.

He brought them to the Bishop who had Required a proof that the request to build A church was authentic. A miraculous Image of Our Lady of Guadalupe was Imprinted on his rough tilma as proof.

Shortly after she appeared, nine million Indians embraced the Catholic faith.

The Immaculate Virgin, Mother of God Endearingly called Juan Diego, "Smallest And most beloved of my sons."...

Our Immaculate and Beautiful Virgin Mary, the Mother of Jesus, is our kind, loving and compassionate mother who was given to us all when Jesus was dying on the cross. She helped end the yearly sacrifice of thousands of victims whose hearts were torn out and offered to the sun.

Our Lady of Guadalupe came not only for the Americas, but for the entire world to bring all of God's children to worship the true Son of God, present with us now in the Holy Eucharist till the end of time, which is drawing near.

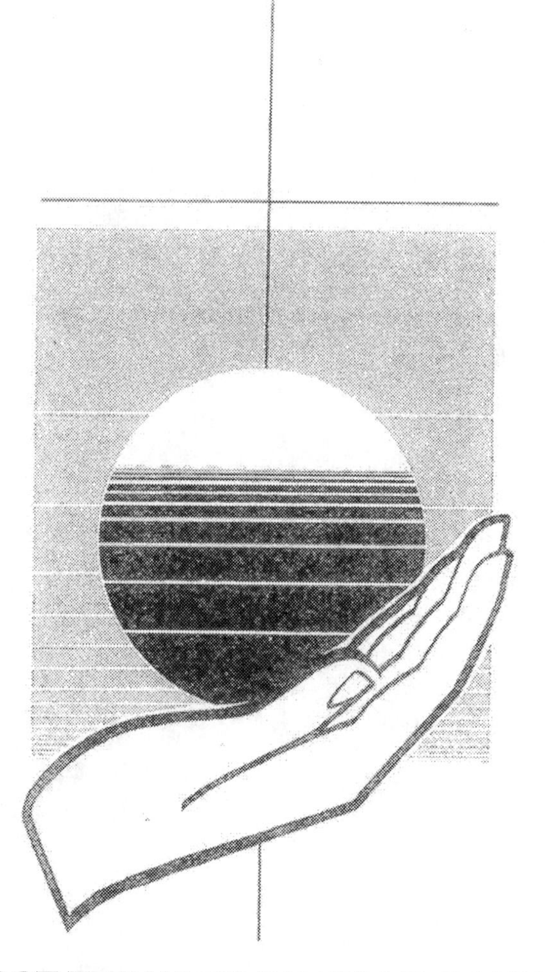

HE'S GOT THE WHOLE WORLD IN HIS HANDS

HAS RESTORED
EDEN

WE DISCOVER
THE JOY
OF A
LITTLE BABY

GOD VEILING
HIMSELF

REJOICE
IN THE
ADORATION
OF THE
LIVING BREAD
FROM HEAVEN

AGAIN...

GOD

VEILING HIMSELF

LAUGHTER

HAPPY BIRTHDAY JESUS

Every day is Christmas for one who is in love with Jesus in the Holy Eucharist.

"There is nothing so great, my children, as the Eucharist." St. John Vianney, The Cure of Ars

"There are three things that are real: God, human folly and laughter. The first two are beyond our comprehension, so we must do what we can with the third." President John F Kennedy

"God is the Creator of Laughter that is Good." Philo

There are only Seven Sacraments in the Catholic Church. So suppose there were Eight instead. Would it not be Joy, Laughter, and Humor to help us get through the Sufferings of Life for they too are treasured and precious gifts from Our loving God of Surprises and Humor.

WITH GRATITUDE

For my beautiful Bride Jacinta, and our beloved daughters, Joy Christie and Juanita for their love and devotedness. My wonderful parents, Julius and Nellie Di Cresce of blessed memory. For my dear sisters, Louise, Dolores and my brother, the saintly Deacon Eugene, (may he rest in peace).

For the great Fr. Tony Wilwerding who is a treasured member of our family. For the great Father Venantius Preske, my spiritual director, who first suggested writing this book. I call it, "Jesus' Book."

I will be forever grateful to the SCJ's, the Priests and Brothers of the Sacred Heart of Jesus for all that I received from them and for daily adoration of the Holy Eucharist in the spirit of love and reparation.

For Sister Bridget O'Neill, IWBS, a dear 100-year-old nun who I met when I was a sailor in Corpus Christ, Texas in World War II and has faithfully prayed for me all these years. For Johnny Sartin, a man of peace and his incredible contributions and help.

For Dolores Gorton whose life is centered on Jesus and has been genuinely helpful with her loving support, prayers and skills. I treasure her wisdom and judgment. Dolores kept saying that "it was our Lord's work, who has truly anointed it, blessed it and is behind it all."

For Debbie MacGregor, who has been so generous and supportive, and is a great woman. Behind every great man is a great woman. Our beloved pastor, Fr. Thomas C. Marks has two secretaries greatly devoted to our Church, Becky and Diana, and all our wonderful and special Saint Michael the Archangel Church family. For my Brothers, Jim Hill, Gerry Stehno, and the men at our Saturday Morning Study/Prayer Group who are simply awesome in our mutual sharing.

FOR OUR DEAR Mother Mary Teresa of Jesus and her holy community of Carmelite cloistered nuns in Valparaiso, Nebraska who are genuine family to us and have continuously prayed for our family and for this book. They have many young women joining them and are starting a new foundation in Elysburg, PA. We are also blessed to have Mother Marie Therese's and her Carmelite cloistered contemplative nuns of Jefferson City, Missouri for their many prayers. For my Sisters-in-law, Frances Baca and Cathy Garcia who graciously helped, and Irene Barrack who is ardently devoted to Jesus in the Holy Eucharist and was most supportive. There are so many others too numerous to mention. You know who you are.

<u>AND TO YOU DEAR READER WHOM GOD LOVES SO MUCH</u>

I thank God for you all... May you come to have or already have a deep faith and devotion for Jesus who is truly in the Holy Eucharist and a love for our Beautiful Blessed Mother Mary and the Great St. Joseph. May you become devoted and faithful Eucharistic Saints to help turn this upside-down world right side up!

A NEW LIFE… A NEW WORLD

Who would have imagined, dreamt or come up with the idea that such a thing could ever have happened?

To love someone so much as to give oneself as food, as bread… so overwhelming is the love and desire to become one.

Lord, if we believe your word, then love and prayer is all powerful and the means to make one's life and this world completely new.

You said: *"Come to me, all of you who are weary and find life burdensome, and I will refresh you. Take my yoke upon your shoulders and learn from me, for I am gentle and humble of heart."* Matthew 11:29

We come to You in the Holy Eucharist to know You, be with You and grow in faith and friendship so we can say,

"It is no longer I who live, but Christ who lives in me."
Galatians 2:20

We want to imitate You so we can go about radiating You and becoming the New Person you have always wanted us to be.

Lord, You have a special plan for each one of us. We will be astounded with joy because of our New Life in You and a New World in the making.

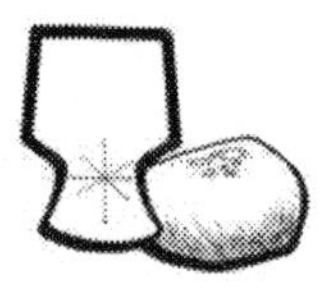

If you are the Son of God, give us the living bread of eternal life so we can live forever.

"Truly, Truly I say to you before Abraham was, I am."

John 8:56

THE SONG OF JESUS

"Truly, truly, I say to you, it was not Moses who gave you bread from heaven for the bread of God is that which comes down from heaven, and gives life to the world."

John 6:32-33

"Truly, truly, I say to you, he who believes has eternal life. I am the bread of life. Your fathers ate the manna in the wilderness, and they died. This is the bread which comes down from heaven, that a man may eat of it and not die. I am the living bread which came down from heaven; if anyone eats of this bread, he will live forever; and the bread which I shall give for the life of the world is my flesh."

John 6:48-51

"THIS IS INDEED THE PROPHET WHO IS TO COME INTO THE WORLD!"

John 6:14

I AM THE BREAD OF LIFE

BE NOT AFRAID...GOD LOVES YOU...HE IS PRESENT AND IS ALWAYS WITH YOU IN THE HOLY EUCHARIST

Christ is the Word of Life
Come, let us adore Him.

"The unique and indivisible existence of the Lord glorious in heaven is not multiplied, but is rendered present by the sacrament in the many places on earth where Mass is celebrated. And this existence remains present, after the sacrifice, in the Blessed Sacrament which is in the tabernacle, the living heart of each of our churches. And it is our very sweet duty to honor and adore in the blessed Host which our eyes see, the Incarnate Word whom they cannot see, and who, without leaving heaven, is made present before us."

Pope Paul VI, The Credo of the People of God

"I am the bread of life; he who comes to me shall not hunger and he who believes in me shall never thirst." John 6:35

A MODERN PARABLE

A Robber entered the grocery store with his hand in one pocket and held out a bag with the other hand.

"Empty the cash register and fill up the bag."

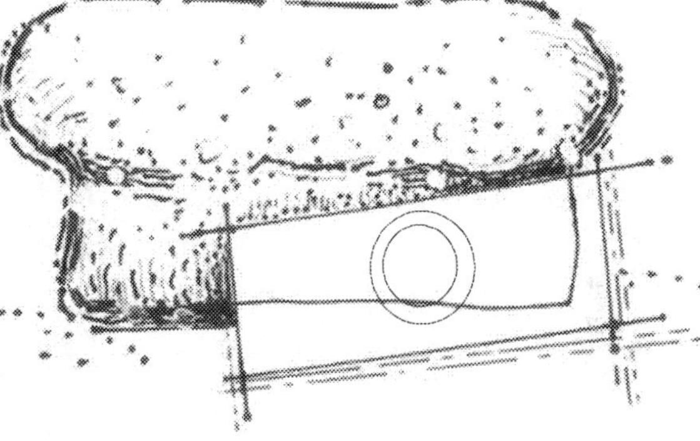

The clerk grabbed his hidden automatic rifle, pointing it at the Robber.

The frightened intruder fell to his knees pleading for mercy.

Sobbing, he cried out, *"Don't shoot... please... I don't want to be a thief and I don't have a gun... it was just my hand. I lost my job. We have no money. My family is starving. Have mercy... please!"*

Feeling sorry for him, the clerk gave him a loaf of bread and some money.

The Robber was overwhelmed and grateful.

The Bread is a reminder that our Lord gives Himself to us in the Holy Eucharist. He gives not money but the true riches that will never fail.

If you, I and all the Nations will begin to take the first step to practice forgiveness and kindness with giving, sharing and serving... will it not begin to help rebuild a New World of Peace and Brotherly Unity?

For love overcomes everything.
Love accomplishes the impossible.

My Friend,

In the beginning of the
Book I shared with you
That I actually experienced
The presence of God in the
Holy Eucharist.

<u>IT IS ALL TRUE.</u>

He who is the *Living Bread from Heaven*, is our Lord and Savior God
Who is truly in the Holy Eucharist.

One day may the world discover
That the Eucharist is the ultimate
Reality of true and genuine love.

One day may we all be one and
Rejoice merrily together with
God in the green pastures of
Our homeland in Heaven.

May our Beautiful Mother Mary
And the Great St. Joseph pray that
Every one will receive the gift of Faith,
Hope and Charity to believe and
Be faithfully devoted to God in
The Holy Eucharist... and to
Love one another.

peter paul

Worship the Lord with the Beauty of a Holy Life

"God became a Little Child to give us an encouraging example on how to live and to be one with Him and with one another in Simplicity, Forgiveness and Love. He and He alone... is the Hope and answer to all the World's problems. We need to know ourselves and strive to seek Truth... otherwise we are simply spinning our wheels.

A JOYFUL COVENANT

Jesus foresaw it all...
Throughout the Ages.
All the sins, all
The horrors of
Diabolical evils and
Unbelievable suffering
Of His beloved and treasured
Children whose first Parents
Were lied to and deceived
By the one who promised:

"You will be like God." Genesis 3:5

Only the Sacrificial Lamb
Of God, the Messiah, Holy
Image of the Father, who
Alone could restore the
Original Innocence, Goodness
And Love lost in the Garden
Of Paradise.

Oh my Father, I Your
Beloved Son, offer restoration
And much more, by dying
On the Cross of Calvary and
Becoming the Eucharistic Bread,
Your precious gift of the
New Covenant of Joyful
Eternal Life... Forever and Ever.

Hope is what we need
most today. Jesus'
generosity is unbelievable.

If Jesus can feed
thousands with only
five loaves of bread
and two fishes...
How much more then
will He do for you?

BUT THERE IS ONLY ONE

There are thousands and thousands of
Myriad flowers in the meadows...
There are thousands of honey bees
Gathering pollen from beautiful flowers.
There are thousands of wonderful winged
Butterflies fluttering with sweet nectar...
There are thousands of colorful birds
Warbling joyful songs of heavenly praise...
There are billions of glittering
Stars in the heavens above...
And there are millions of Adorers
Of Jesus in His Sacrament of Love.

**But there is only... One... Beautiful,
Holy and Immaculate... Virgin Mary...**

THE BLESSED MOTHER OF GOD...
YOUR MOTHER AND MINE.
JESUS GAVE HER TO US WHEN HE
WAS ON THE CROSS OF CALVARY
AND NOW SHE BRINGS US
TO JESUS IN THE MOST HOLY
EUCHARIST, THE SACRAMENT
OF LOVE, AND SHE HELPS US
ON OUR JOURNEY TO THE
GREEN PASTURES IN HEAVEN
ABOVE AS WE HELP ALL SOULS
TO BECOME SAINTS OF GOODNESS
AND OF ETERNAL JOYFUL LOVE.

"This is my beloved Son, with
whom I am well pleased;
listen to him." Matthew 17:5

EUCHARIST PRAYERS

O Jesus living in Mary,
Tabernacle of Christ the Messiah
O Jesus/ Eucharist, Life of my soul,
Come and live in Your servants,
In the spirit of Your own holiness,
In the fullness of Your power,
In the reality of Your virtues,
In the perfection of Your ways,
In the communion of Your mysteries,
Have dominion over every adverse power,
In Your own spirit,
To the glory of the Father.
Amen.

Adapted from Jean Jacques Olier's Prayer
Founder of Seminary and Society of
St. Sulpice 1608-1657

IN the Eucharist the Church is completely united to Christ and his sacrifice, and makes her own the spirit of Mary. This truth can be understood more deeply by *re-reading the Magnificat* in a Eucharistic key. The Eucharist, like the Canticle of Mary, is first and foremost praise And thanksgiving. When Mary exclaims: "My Sou magnifies the Lord and my spirit rejoices In God my Saviour," She already bears Jesus In her womb. She praises God "Through" Jesus, but she also praises him "in" Jesus and "with" Jesus. This is itself the true "Eucharistic Attitude."

Ecclesia de Eucharistia Ioannes Paulus PP.II
Ch. 6, No. 58

My soul magnifies the Lord,
and my spirit rejoices in God my Savior;
For he has regarded the lowliness of
his handmaid; for, behold, henceforth all
generations shall call me blessed;
Because he who is mighty has done great things
for me, and holy is his name;
And his mercy is from generation
to generation on those who fear him.
He has shown might with his arm, he has scattered
the proud in the conceit of their heart.
He has put down the mighty from their
thrones, and has exalted the lowly.
He has filled the hungry with good things,
and the rich he has sent away empty.
He has given help to Israel, his servant,
Mindful of his mercy
According to the promise he made to our ancestors
To Abraham and to his descendants forever.

Luke 1: 46-55

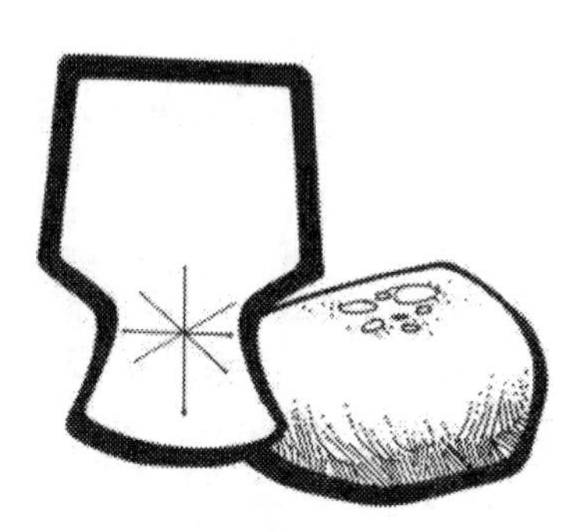

IT IS A CALL TO LOVE

JOYFUL MIRROR OF CHRIST

"Even in the modern world St. Francis Of Assisi is one of the most popular And admired of the saints. He is also One of the most misunderstood. But There was one modern writer who Understood him well...

"In his wonderful book (St. Francis Of Assisi), G. K. Chesterton describes St. Francis first as a soldier and a Fighter. Then as a builder and a Reformer. Then as a jester, a clown Of God, a troubadour, and a poet. Then as a beggar, who embraced Poverty as other men embrace Wealth, a poor little man, who Embraced not only all men as his Brothers, but all creatures great And small. And finally, Chesterton Describes Frances as a mirror of Christ, one who reflected the light Of truth."

G.K. CHESTERTON, THE APOSTLE OF COMMON SENSE
By Dale Ahlquist, Pg. 91-92
Ignatius Press, San Francisco

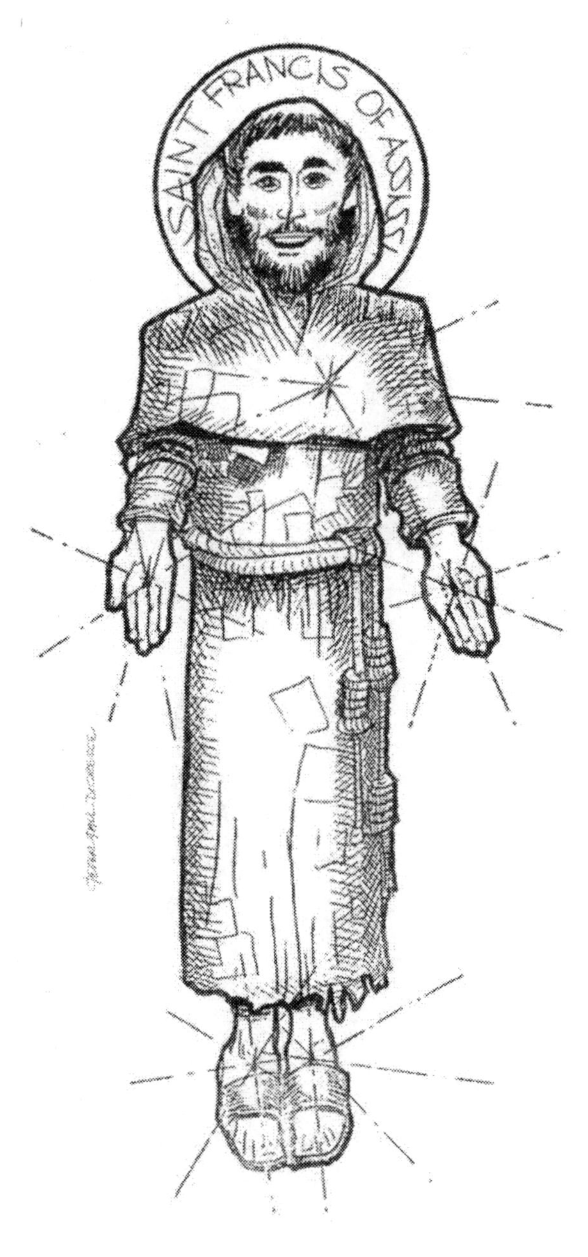

May you too always
mirror the Light of Christ!

TO ORDER

Eucharist MIRACLE OF ALL MIRACLES... LOVE OF ALL LOVES

CALL TOLL FREE: 1 (888) 232-4444
FROM CANADA OR USA

INTERNATIONAL: (000) 250-383-6864

OR WRITE:

TRAFFORD PUBLISHING
1663 LIBERTY DRIVE
SUITE 200
BLOOMINGTON, INDIANA 47403
UNITED STATES OF AMERICA

OR

ORDER FROM YOUR
LOCAL BOOK STORE